CHINA TRIUMPHS

Other Books by J. A. del Vayo

Freedom's Battle

The Last Optimist

Alemania

La Nueva Rusia

La Senda Roja

CHINA TRIUMPHS

Julio Alvarez del Vayo

translated from the Spanish

by

William Rose

MR

Monthly Review Press
New York

68- 3937

Copyright © 1964
by Julio Alvarez del Vayo

Manufactured in the U.S.A.

Library of Congress catalog card number 64-23144

Published by Monthly Review Press
333 Sixth Avenue, New York 14, N. Y.

 357

Contents

Contents

1

REFLECTIONS EN ROUTE

The airplane that should have taken us from Moscow to Peking in eleven hours ran into a heavy overcast and bad weather in Siberia that held us up for three days. During this delay I found my thoughts often flying ahead of me to the country of my destination, and I relived some of the experiences of my previous visit to China in 1957, four years before.

From that visit there remained imprinted on my memory a double impression: one of the most daring and imaginative revolutionary undertakings of our time combined with a constant homage to the past—a past which has produced the richest and most varied civilization in the world. Perhaps a symbol of this union is the fact that China's chief revolutionary leader, Mao Tse-tung, is a poet. Scholars or scientists who are not members of the Communist Party are treated with the same esteem that was accorded learned men in the days of the oldest dynasties—assuming, of course, that the non-Party intellectuals are not opposed to the objectives of the Revolution.

I recalled my emotion when our interpreter in Chengtu showed us the temple honoring Liu Pang, the great ruler during the Han dynasty. It was under his patronage that an ingenious irrigation project, conceived over 2,200 years ago, was completed. This project served as a point of departure for the recent hydraulic development of the area.

My visit to Chungking was as vivid in my memory as if I had been there a few hours previously. There I had visited the Room of the Five Hundred Buddhas, unique in this world. I could still hear the voice of the monk who showed it to us. "Today the government respects us," he said, and he proceeded to tell us sadly how the soldiers of Chiang Kai-shek treated with absolute scorn the community's Buddhist sentiments, leaving the temples in a ruined state after having utilized them as barracks.

The paintings in the temples alone would justify a trip to Chengtu and Chungking. Another monk, a historian and evidently an artist, pointed out the contrast between the policy of China today and the negligence of the rulers of the last dynasty, under which the country was despoiled of many precious art objects.

The plunder tolerated by the bureaucrats of the old regime, under the guise of "scientific expeditions" perpetrated by foreigners who were externally of the most respectable sort, was tremendous. As a single instance, my guide recalled the visit of the Englishman, Sir Aurel Stein, to Sinkiang at the beginning of this century. Sir Aurel had learned of the great artistic wealth of that province, and Sinkiang received him with open arms as an enthusiast of the Buddhist philosophy and tradition. Introducing himself to the monk who guarded the famous Crypts of Tunhuang—450 vaults containing priceless collections of Chinese art dating back to the second century B.C.—Sir Aurel explained that he had a "divine mission" to make known throughout Asia the strength of the moral teachings of Buddhism, and that he was to accomplish this mission by launching a traveling exhibition of the treasures of the Crypts of Tunhuang. Not long after, these treasures were to be found in the museums of Britain and other countries and in private collections.

In Shanghai I had spent several evenings with the artists of the Peking Opera. I had met the great actor, Mei Lan-fang, who, at 64, electrified the audience with his interpretation of the roles of the loveliest heroines of Chinese legend. Mei Lan-fang died shortly after I saw him perform, but I could still see before me his exquisite femininity in the part of a woman and his virile, incredibly young presence offstage as he explained what the government of Chou En-lai was doing to make opera and ballet the best that China could offer.

A newspaperman all my adult life, with the virus of journalism in my veins, I had made it a point to visit the offices of the newspaper publishers. Through my contacts with reporters I had learned much about life in China which had escaped me in my talks with other people. The quantity of correspondence Chinese dailies receive from their readers is astounding. This is true of both cities and the provinces. There are more than 300 periodicals, 18 of which are distributed nationally, including, of course, *Jenmin Jih Pao* (*The People's Daily*, official organ of the Chinese Communist Party). Particularly exciting for me was a visit to a compositor's room, where I watched the champion of the year—a woman—at work. Her flying fingers had beaten the record of 2,500 characters set per hour.

I recalled each Chinese city I had visited. There was Changchun (which means "eternal spring" in Chinese) in beautiful Manchuria, with its innumerable trees and gardens, known already in 1957 as the "city of the automobile." Then, there was Anshan, the "city of steel," where I became convinced that the delays in China's industrialization effort, caused by the need to give priority to agriculture, would not prevent China from becoming some day a major industrial power. Shanghai, perhaps more than any other Chinese city, invited comparison between the modern methods of production and the old ones. For in Shanghai there is a great number and variety of factories, workshops, and enterprises of all kinds.

Canton, I learned, means "ample"; and it is, indeed, a city of large proportions as well as one of the oldest cities in China. I could not easily forget the view of the port from the balcony of the "Hotel of the Love of the Masses." The panorama embraced hundreds of delightful Chinese boats, flying flags of gold stars on a red background. Some of the larger boats served as dwellings for a constantly increasing population.

Perhaps my favorite memory, however, was of Peking in April. There I had come to know the Chinese spring with its flowers and birds, looking so much like the paintings by Chao Kie and the Emperor Hui Tsung of the Sung dynasty—and looking so much, too, like modern Chinese paintings, for everything in the New China is interwoven with and related to the past. The revolutionary and the classical are joined.

How well I recalled the men and women I had met on my first visit—from Mao Tse-tung to the young man who ran the night elevator at my hotel and who never seemed in the least surprised to see me leave my hotel in the middle of the night to walk alone in the streets of Peking. I remembered the revered

Madame Sun Yat-sen, sister of Madame Chiang Kai-shek (never could two sisters be more different!) and the working girl in Hangchow who explained to me in English, more effectively than any sociology professor could have done, what the Revolution in China had meant for women.

All these memories increased my pleasure at the prospect of returning to China and aroused a sort of professional pride in my mission to discover and to tell some of the truth about modern China to those left in ignorance or deceived by misinformation. I also had the feeling that I was returning to the country which, more than any other, would be on everybody's lips in the remaining years of this century.

My pleasant recollections of China and my sense of anticipation on returning did not absorb me totally during my unexpectedly long trip from Moscow to Peking. I also found time to do some studying. Since I knew that a knowledge of Chinese geography, however summary, was indispensable to an understanding of the problems and accomplishments of the New China, I spent some hours pouring over geography books.

China is the third largest country in the world, after the Soviet Union and Canada. Her continental borders extend more than 9,300 miles. In addition, four great seas bathe her shores. Her landscape includes some of the most awesome mountain peaks on the face of the earth as well as vast areas of plains. The diversity of climate permits one in the same month of the year to enjoy spring in Canton and the spectacle of trees covered with frost in Peking. Though this diversity assures a great variety of flora and fauna, it also has its drawbacks. The coastal regions are exposed to typhoons, and other vast regions to droughts and floods.

The great rivers of China are a source of wealth—but also of violence. The Yangtze, greatest of them all, is more than 3,400 miles long. Altogether, China's rivers provide more than 62,000 miles of navigable waterways, of which 18,600 miles are accessible to steamboats.

China's largest cities—Shanghai, Wuhan, Canton, Chungking, Nanking—are located in the Southeast, but the Northeast is the center of large industry. The most heavily populated region

in China is the lower Yangtze basin; here live 78 million people
—500 inhabitants per square mile. The natural conditions of
the region caused the peasantry to move there long ago. They
were soon followed by the artisans and the merchants. As foreign
penetration extended, businessmen from outside moved in with
their offices and banks. In addition to being a center for
agriculture, business, and industry, the Yangtze region is also
quite rich in iron ore.

The coast of Southeast China includes three provinces:
Chekiang, Fukien, and Kwangtung. Here a warm, damp climate
produces abundant vegetation, including subtropical trees, tea
and bamboo. Rice crops are harvested twice a year. Fukien,
whose cedars are highly prized everywhere, is also a center of
the Chinese fishing industry and of sugar refining.

South China is famous for the rice fields along the Pearl
River. The South China Sea, largest of the Chinese seas, provides
a great variety of tropical fish. Kwangtung and Kwangsi are
rich in non-ferrous metals. And Canton, the principal city in
Kwangtung province, is known for its new silk industries and
the fascination of its crowded harbor.

Yunnan touches Laos and Vietnam on the south and Burma
on the west. Gigantic waterfalls and torrential rains wash its
mountains and valleys. Its prodigious fauna include enormous
bears, elephants, apes, as well as other feared wild animals—
creatures that used to be a constant threat to the crops and
those who cultivated them. At present Yunnan enjoys a rising
agricultural economy.

The Szechwan region, center of West China, is particularly
fertile, thanks to the mild climate and the structure of the soil.
Almost all crops can be grown there, from corn to sweet potatoes.

Sinkiang, the autonomous Uighur Republic, can expect a
rich and expanding future. It touches the Soviet Union on one
side and the Mongolian People's Republic on the other. In the
Tarim basin the climate is dry, the summer short and the winters
prolonged and glacial. The climatic differences between the
mountain region and the lowlands affect crop distribution and
vegetation. The pine forests of the Altai are known throughout
the country. There is an abundance of medicinal plants and of

animals which provide a flourishing fur industry. Great mineral
resources of all kinds—oil, coal, iron, gold, jade—are only now
beginning to be exploited. Particularly rich in oil is the Karamai
region.

I was deep in my geographic "cramming" when we began
to see from the plane the outlines of the agricultural installations
near Peking which I intended to visit. This was an eagerly
awaited moment. Soon we would land and start our second
visit to a country in which one can observe one of the greatest
manifestations of this century of the creative power of the masses.
The attraction of China comes only in part from the beauty of its
landscape and from contact with people who reveal in their
ways the wisdom and refinement of the oldest civilization on
earth. For, in addition, one can watch them in the very act of
forging the history of tomorrow, despite great obstacles. Moreover, one feels the attraction of a country which is little understood in its present phase, even by many who acclaimed the
successes of the first years of the Revolution.

In the Peking airport we met our friends from the Institute
of Foreign Affairs and left with them, discussing the incidents of
the trip. Suddenly we saw a great building which we did not
recognize, which we could not have recognized, because it wasn't
there in 1957. It was the first sign of the changes that had
occurred in China in the four years since my previous visit.

2

PEKING

Grand Palace of the People and Museum of History

Between 1957 and 1961 Peking had grown considerably. In the city's vast central plaza, called Tien An Men, two new buildings stood out strikingly—the Grand Palace of the People (China's Parliament), with a capacity of 10,000 persons, and the Historical Museum of China. Both were constructed in only ten months. Massive and handsome, they disprove the frequent charge that in China today buildings are erected quickly but poorly.

The main hall of the Grand Palace of the People is immense and very beautiful at the same time. Each of the rooms, which compete in originality, is the gift of one of the major provinces to the supreme representative body of the Chinese people. In the one presented by Chungking province we admired a large bamboo portiere with bas-reliefs depicting the hydraulic projects of the New China. The room donated by Canton province contains ivory and ceramics.

The banquet hall is of impressive dimensions. There is marble everywhere, some of it a very attractive greenish color, and rugs worthy of the famous tradition of Chinese tapestry. In one room a mural, the collective work of several modern painters, illustrates a poem by Mao Tse-tung. Also on view are marvelous jade pieces, a large world globe of onyx, and a lively mural showing the transformation of agriculture between the time the new regime took power and the establishment of the People's Communes.

I know of no parliament in the world which meets in such a hall. It is like a synthesis of the work done throughout the country in Chinese architectural art. Perhaps the most difficult achievement has been the tasteful combination of grandeur and exquisite detail.

In front of this building rises the Museum of History, with exhibits covering the period from the first appearance of human society in China about 500,000 years ago to the year 1840, when the struggle began against foreign invasion and the domination of Western imperialism. It records three phases of Chinese development: primitive clans, slavery, and feudalism.

These two buildings demonstrate the important role which architecture plays in the New China. There are two different schools of thought among Chinese architects: one maintains that materials and structural methods are what determine style, while the other holds that, even though these factors are important, what mainly determines style is social ideology. Professor Liang Sze-cheng, director of the faculty of architectural engineering of Tsinghua University, shares the latter opinion. He reached that conclusion after making a comparative study of ancient Chinese architecture and that of Western countries.

"Having in his hands new materials and new techniques," says Professor Liang, "man should control them, not be at their service. Our task is to understand and to dominate materials and techniques and make them play the most complete role possible in regard to function, structure, economy, and beauty." And he emphasizes the development in China of a new architectural style, samples of which are the great new buildings in Peking, the monument to the writer, Lu Hsun, in Shanghai, some recent buildings in the city of Hsinhui in Kwangtung province, and the pavilions at the ends of the bridge over the Yangtze at Wuhan. "These reflect," he insists, "the combative spirit of the Chinese people and their determination in the construction of socialism."

But there is no rupture with the past. Professor Liang adds: "On analyzing and studying ancient architecture in all its details, we find that some of the materials and methods of applying them can be useful today. However, we must absorb, with critical discrimination, not only our own architectural tradition, but also everything of value in foreign architecture."

The Grand Stadium

Another innovation in Peking is the Grand Stadium, built to satisfy the desire of the workers in the capital for a sports palace on the order of Canton's. Erected under the direction of the Draftsmen's Institute in Peking its total surface covers almost 100 acres. The central field alone holds 100,000 spectators and at night the 380 lighting units make a magnificent spectacle of this field. The Chinese are masters of lighting and they have made a true work of art out of the lighting in the Grand Stadium.

An artificial lake permits rowing in the summer and skating in the winter. The temperature in the swimming pools is regulated in such a way that swimming contests need not depend on the whims of the weather. To swim in a heated pool costs the worker only a few cents.

The Stadium—with its living units for the athletes who come from the provinces to take part in contests, its tracks for bicycle races, its fields for football, acrobatics, discus-throwing, and other sports—reflects the extraordinary interest in athletics which naturally spreads as the general standard of living rises. It is estimated that more than a million workers visit the Stadium regularly during the course of a year—as active participants, not spectators.

The world championship ping-pong matches were held recently in the covered area. Table tennis occupies one of the first places in sports in China today. No one has yet been able to defeat the male teams, and the female teams are training determinedly to reach the level set by the men. The Japanese and the Hungarians are the main competition for the Chinese in this sport.

The Stadium is located on a site which was only waste land at the time of our first visit to China. Now it is serving one of the main purposes of the Health Program. "Without the concern for health which has been growing in the Chinese people every year since the Liberation, the construction of the Stadium would have been inconceivable," the director told us. We had a lively conversation with him and his aides about the current state of sports on the national level.

The Central Station

The fourth great building constructed during our absence was the new Peking Central Railway Station. The old station is now used for union festivals. In it we saw a performance by the railway workers, as skilled in acrobatics as they are in running their trains.

We saw many Chinese from overseas get off the express that brought us from Shanghai. The sight of the new Peking station evidently made them very happy, for they did not try to hide their emotion. Such visitors, particularly from Hong Kong, come frequently now to visit the New China. During the holiday seasons—Christmas, the Chinese New Year, May Day, the anniversary of the Revolution (October 1)—the number of Chinese visitors coming from Hong Kong, according to a statement by the mayor of Canton, reaches 1,000 a day. Normally, the number is about 500 daily.

One who arrives at the station with time to spare need not be bored, because several mobile libraries offer free and varied reading. This is just one more way to spread culture—one way among many. For in China all possible means are employed to disseminate learning throughout the country. I was informed, for example, that about 35,000 students were taking television courses conducted by the University of Peking. The courses dealt with Chinese language and literature, mathematics, physics, chemistry, and the preparatory program for the institutes and universities. Those advancing their education by television included government employees, miners and factory workers, teachers, army officers and soldiers, and officials of the People's Communes.

The new station in Peking is not only beautiful but very practical. Its 17 waiting rooms, with a total capacity of 17,000 persons, accommodate a population which is acquiring more of a taste for travel with every year that goes by. Each important train has a waiting room adjoining its platform, and the rooms reserved for mothers and their children have received special attention; mothers find it easy to entertain their children in these rooms and there are nurses handy to cope with any emergency.

Every waiting room has a telephone connection with the station's information office, thus eliminating the shoving, impatient crowds of passengers one sees clustered around the information desks of stations in other countries.

Pei-hai Park

Peking has been enriched in recent years with two new parks and with avenues which have been built at the expense of tearing down parts of the ancient city wall—though this has been done as sparingly as possible. Whenever there is no other program, Sunday is the day to visit the parks, no matter in what city one may be. We were already familiar with many parks, but had not yet seen the one most enjoyed by the people— the Pei-hai or Winter Park, constructed in the tenth century when it was part of the reigning dynasty's palace area. Its white pagoda is of more "modern" construction, dating from 1651. After 1925 the palace and grounds were converted into a public park, but it is only recently that it has become a favorite recreation spot.

We strolled around the lake, where preparations for an improvised regatta were going on, to the gallery of the Buddhas, where statues of the Buddha, each with a completely different expression from the others, are lined up in the recently restored temple. Some visitors to the gallery carried small volumes—not prayer books but art guides. And in the park's reading room, just as in the main station, many people were poring over newspapers and magazines.

On leaving the library an old man with a long, very thin beard, an impressive survivor of an ancient society incorporated into a new one, looked at us insistently. He knew English and we spoke to him. Suddenly he made an obviously deeply felt observation. "In China everyone knows why he is working and for whom he is working." We learned that he was a craftsman in one of the jade and ivory workshops.

There is no important Chinese park without its aquarium. The variety of fish is extraordinary, and in this one we admired above all the pearl fish with their many-colored scales. Small children pushed through the crowd to see them. Some of these children had no doubt spent the whole day in the park. If parents have work to do or must attend a meeting, the children are taken to the park in the morning, left in the care of nurses provided by the administration, and picked up in the evening. Between games, the children ride around in little transparent carriages that are as beautiful as their passengers, who resemble porcelain dolls.

Reforestation

Seeing Peking from the top of the hill, one is impressed by the great number of trees. Nine million new ones were planted in this city alone, under a plan for urban improvement and reforestation which will provide the double benefit of fruit and the wood so necessary for the construction of new housing. Later on, in visits to other major Chinese cities I remarked the same profusion of fruit trees. I have seen them flourish in the most unexpected places—audaciously planted, for example, on formerly bare mountains.

Within a few years, the reforestation policy will assure China a preponderant position as a wood-exporting country, although domestic needs will absorb a considerable part of lumber production. In the great mountains of Khingan in northeastern China, which contain one fifth of the nation's wood resources, not only have great numbers of young trees been planted, but mechanization has been introduced on a large scale in felling the trees and dragging them to the nearest transportation point.

But the cultivation of large trees of a positive utilitarian value does not imply the sacrifice of the small trees immortalized in Chinese painting. These survive in some mysterious way in the midst of the incessant growth of the city.

Transportation and Public Services

At the end of the nineteenth century the only means of locomotion for the non-privileged inhabitant of Peking was his legs, and his transportation problem had still not been solved under the government of Chiang Kai-shek. In fact, just before the Liberation, the capital, which then had a population of about two million, possessed only 49 streetcars and five motor busses. Eight years later, at the time of our first visit, it had more than 60 motor bus lines and 10 trolley bus lines. In 1961 Peking had 73 motor bus lines and 13 trolley bus lines, while taxis were also beginning to appear on the streets. A thousand automobiles, most of them of Chinese make, helped somewhat. But the transportation problem is still critical, especially when great numbers of delegations and individuals are visiting the city.

Incidentally, the appearance of a Chinese automobile, which has a very good design and motor, made us recall that in 1957, in the great tractor factory of Changchun where the cars are made, we were told that no automobiles would be produced until 1962. But at the beginning of 1961 they were already rolling off the line. This is what is lost sight of in certain commentaries on the industrialization of this country. In some branches of production the rate may have diminished, but in others it has steadily accelerated.

A constant improvement in state services is apparent. The traffic police, the only police to be seen, control traffic which formerly was far less orderly.

The postal service is very good. Aside from the more than 300 offices in the capital itself and in the most important surrounding districts, each hotel has its own postal and telegraph service. I received my correspondent's telegraph credentials as soon as I applied for them and I found a radio in my room on which I could follow last-minute world news.

In this connection, I must mention the charming girl in the post office of the Hotel Peking who always took care that the stamps she put on the letters I mailed were as varied as possible for the pleasure of those who received them. Chinese stamps, with their flowers, birds, and landscapes, are a collector's delight.

In Peking one can take a walk at any time of night without being bothered by anyone. In comparison to Paris, with its nocturnal assaults and Madrid, where beggars do not leave the pedestrians in peace, this represents definite progress. One does not have to be afraid of getting lost, either. It is rare to find a completely deserted street. The continuity of work shifts assures a constant flow of people, some going to work and others returning home. And a stranger has only to show a piece of paper with his address written in Chinese and there will be a friendly, smiling Chinese who will show him the way and, if necessary, accompany him to his destination.

Role of Women

Article 96 of the Constitution of the People's Republic stipulates: "Women in the People's Republic of China enjoy equal rights with men in all areas of political, cultural, social and family life. The State protects marriage, the family, mothers, and children."

As a consequence of this provision, more than 12 percent of the members of the National People's Assembly are women. One of the vice presidents of the Republic is Soong Ching-ling (Mme. Sun Yat-sen). Among the vice presidents of the Permanent Committee of the National People's Assembly is a woman —Ho Hsiang-ning; in addition, four of the Committee members are women.

In the Central People's Government, seven ministers and vice ministers are women, and there is one woman, Li Chen, among the generals of the people's Army of Liberation.

Of the scientific workers under the Academy of Sciences of China—the supreme research organization for the whole country—22 percent are women. In the hospitals an increasing number of women doctors are holding administrative positions. The same is true of museums, libraries and schools, including the normal schools which train the nation's teachers.

We have found women in charge of the most diverse organizations within the country and in diplomatic missions abroad. But women at the head of important industrial enterprises were unusual even a few years ago. Now, however, their services are being utilized more and more in this field, a fact that was brought home to us when we met the very capable Tung Chan-su, director of the Peking Coking Chemical Plant.

This is one of the industrial enterprises organized as part of the Great Leap Forward, which explains why it was finished with such speed. Twelve thousand tons of brick were used in its construction—which gives one an idea of the size of this huge plant which is managed by a woman.

"Made in China"

This factory is one of the first of its kind completely "made in China." That is, it was planned and built by the Chinese and constructed exclusively with Chinese materials. In 1957, during a meal with Western diplomats in Peking, we heard a discussion about the length of time that China would need to learn to walk "on its own feet," without aid from foreign, mainly Soviet, technicians. The opinion among the diplomats was that a number of years would still have to pass. The only contrary view was expressed by the Ambassador from Finland, who insisted that China's ability to master the problems arising from industrialization would require much less time than his colleagues believed.

That the Finnish Ambassador was right is proven by this factory which, at the time I saw it, was producing over 1 1/3 billion cubic feet of gas a year. But supplying gas to the capital is only one of its three functions: the other two are to produce coke (a million tons a year) and to extract from the coke the raw materials—including cooking oil, benzine, and sulphur—necessary for a number of industries.

Tung Chan-su told us of her plans for the future, plans that in themselves were truly ambitious, but which she explained with deliberate caution, as if she already anticipated the readjustment in the rate of industrialization which was to take place a year later. The factory was to supply coke for all the industries of Peking, and gas for its entire population, by 1967.

There seemed to be remarkably few people employed in this enterprise, considering its dimensions and objectives. We learned that there were 3,000 workers and office employees, including 300 women. Such efficiency is probably the result of two combined factors—good management and very young personnel. The average age of the workers was 22 years when I visited the plant. Almost all of the workers were trained in the factory and one had only to watch them to sense the complete confidence they had in themselves, a distinctive characteristic of the young Chinese workers.

"This factory," the director told us, "requires a high degree of mechanization and automation, so that, to fulfill the program which we have outlined, it will not be necessary to increase significantly the number of workers. We have many problems left to solve, however. We still lack the necessary management experience. The engineers in the factory, more than 30 of them, are trying to raise the quality of the work which is still a long way from being perfect. On the other hand, it is true that in comparison with the work done formerly by similar enterprises, it constitutes an advance. . . . That is the important thing, to advance, and in a solid way.

"We encourage workers," she went on, "to imitate the initiative of their most outstanding co-workers. This has certainly improved certain aspects of production. The initiative which the workers have taken to save raw materials, reduce expenses, and increase safety continues to spread. It is like an epidemic of enthusiasm."

Just as in many other places, there are three work shifts in the Peking Coking Chemical Plant. Work continues day after day throughout the year without interruption.

Visits to other factories near Peking reinforced my impression that changes affecting the rate of production—some years moderating its speed, other years increasing it, according to the over-all economic situation—do not alter the basic fact that China already has tooled and organized itself to produce great quantities of things which are indispensable for its national future, things that previously had to be bought abroad with foreign currency.

Let us take the example of locomotives. An engineer told me: "We have succeeded in producing locomotives *en masse*. Steam locomotives may seem out of date to foreigners, but for China, and in comparison with the situation existing only a few years ago, this production constitutes a great advance. Besides, we have already begun to make electric locomotives."

And another engineer said: "For us it is still something extraordinary to realize that our national production taken as a whole already meets 80 percent of China's needs. When I think that when I was a boy not even a bicycle could be made in China! But in addition we are also beginning to export."

To corroborate his statement, I showed him a clipping from

an English newspaper announcing the sale in London of Chinese blouses, and he commented: "Not only blouses, but also the machines that make them! We don't export the machines to England, which has such highly developed textile machinery, but we do to other Asian nations."

One thing is clear: the Chinese government, the Chinese planners, and the Chinese people know perfectly well where they are going. It would be meaningless for me to say: "With the Great Leap Forward they proposed to do this, that, and the other, but they have not succeeded in this or that area of the economy." Such observations do not touch the fundamental fact that China has succeeded in establishing the basis for creating its own economy—an economy that will not be subject to the cruel whims of nature or a changing international situation. Once and for all the Chinese will be able to follow a path which they have laid out for themselves.

Medicine in New China

One of the events we included with pleasure in our Peking program was a visit to Mme. Li Teh-chuan, the Minister of Health.

She received us in the most cordial way imaginable. With her were some of her principal colleagues, among them Dr. Lu Chih-tseng, who is in charge of the formation of medical cadres and who told us about the situation in the main medical schools in the country, and Dr. Chi Chung-po, President of the Academy of Traditional Medicine.

About 100,000 students a year are enrolled in regular courses of study in the various medical schools in China. A great many more, who are following special programs, will leave to take part in the health campaign in the interior and then return later to finish their studies.

"Nevertheless," observed Dr. Lu, "the scarcity of doctors continues. But we are working while 'walking on two legs.' How? First, by combining the efforts of graduate doctors and partially-qualified doctors; and, second, by combining modern medicine with traditional medicine."

The reference to traditional medicine, which involves a

combination treatment of herbs and acupuncture (puncturing of surface skin areas to relieve pain), led to a general discussion of that school of medicine, so deeply rooted in the people.

Madame Li said: "After the Liberation, Chairman Mao insistently recommended that the two schools of medicine be combined, because their cooperation would favor both schools and ultimately the 'great patient'—the people. At that time the Chinese people desperately needed health services. This was the origin of the sanitation campaign about which we talked in my house during your first visit. But since then the campaign has kept growing, because once the epidemics were overcome and the most indispensable sanitary services were established in the country, it was necessary to go into the field of preventive medicine. It is one of the things to which we are giving most attention today.

"Our experience so far, although brief, tells us that we are on the right road. The reports from all parts of the country agree as to the highly favorable results achieved through the use of preventive medicine in urban centers, in factories, in communes. And its success has been greatly aided by cooperation between the two schools of medicine. There were errors in regard to this; I committed them myself."

This last comment was an allusion to certain polemics which are now a thing of the past. There had been a brief period when traditional medicine was frequently denounced as feudal and anti-scientific, while some of its most enthusiastic partisans counter-attacked by accusing "Western" medicine of being "capitalistic" and its practitioners and apologists of being in intellectual servitude to the West.

One must realize that modern medicine, more generally known in China as occidental medicine, has been known there for only a little more than a century. Its introduction in China was accompanied for many years by an absolute lack of co-operation between its practitioners and those of the traditional school.

Today cooperation is the rule. Authorities of both schools, doctors with long years of practice and recent graduates from the medical schools, are interested in developing further a professional association which has proven its value. In one of the hospitals which we visited a few days after our talk with the Minister of Health, several patients suffering from appendicitis were being treated with the traditional methods; in another case, in which there existed the immediate threat of peritonitis, surgery was performed on the recommendation of both traditional and occidental doctors.

Occidental medicine has not ousted traditional medicine from its ancient seat of favor with the Chinese people, nor are its practitioners today interested in doing so. In the last few years traditional medicine has received valuable official aid in expanding its literature, largely through the recovery of ancient texts. The Peking Library, the Institute of Traditional Medicine of Peking, and more than 60 other great provincial libraries cooperated in this task. New editions of ancient classic texts, which had been believed lost, have been printed. Since the Liberation, the publishing house for People's Sanitation of Peking alone has brought out more than 200 titles of traditional medical books, printing a total of over six million copies.

In addition, the establishment in 1956 of the "Twelve Year Plan for Scientific Research" has brought about outstanding progress in the field of individual medical research in both traditional and occidental schools.

Minister Li, as well as her co-workers, insisted, in the course of our conversation, on the need for Chinese doctors to learn from their colleagues abroad, no matter what country they may live in. But some foreign doctors who have been in China recently say they don't have much to teach their Chinese colleagues.

One foreign surgeon, Dr. Sakka, assured us that "the state of Chinese surgery today does not have to envy that of the most advanced Western countries." And he informed us that as early as 1959, heart and vascular surgery was being performed successfully in more than 60 hospitals in China. Out of a homogeneous group of 755 such cases, 81 percent had "very good results." Since 1957, when Chinese surgeons performed the first "open heart" operation, such operations have been performed in 13 provinces, not counting Peking and Shanghai. Vascular surgery on the great arteries has become commonplace in many Chinese hospitals.

"In the handling of heart surgery," concluded Dr. Sakka, "the entire country was divided into seven regions, in each of which the Institute directing the work established a minimum of one cardiological center."

More recent is the testimony of the Canadian surgeon, Professor Wilder Penfield, who was in China in the autumn of 1962. This well-known specialist in neuro-surgery has said that in China operations are performed "as well as they can be performed anywhere in the world." And he declared that he was much honored at having been named a member of the Chinese Medical Association.

Even on one's second trip to China, or on one's third or fourth, one must make "the hospital tour." The hospitals offer a splendid observation center for the person who knows how to look closely. And there is often a new institution that has been built since the last visit, or one which, if not completely new, has been enlarged and brought up to date.

The Peking Children's Hospital is one of the biggest hospitals in China. Its medical staff has increased by 35 percent in the last few years. Since 1958 the Ministry of Sanitation has been organizing courses, increasingly well attended, in Peking and Shanghai for the training of pediatricians. It is not surprising then, that Peking's infant mortality rate has fallen from 117.6 per thousand in 1949 to 29.8 per thousand in 1960. These figures from the Ministry of Sanitation confirmed what we had been told by the administrative personnel of the hospital.

Our visit to Peking's great hospital of traditional medicine, the Secondary Hospital of the Academy of Traditional Medicine, had a double purpose, journalistic and personal. My wife, a native of Switzerland and familiar with the curative qualities of certain herbs, is a believer in Chinese medicine and acupuncture. Drs. Chen Hsiao-tsien and Tung Liang-chen, the principal doctors in the hospital, and among the most noted physicians in the country, expressed great delight at her enthusiasm. Dr. Chen, well past 70, and Dr. Tung, not far from 70, were both vigorous and youthful—striking examples of the virtue of their science.

One could only admire their faces, quite free of wrinkles, their small beards and fine features, like those of the stylized ivory figurines that attract collectors in antique shops.

The directress, who previously served as an army physician, and a young doctor, originally trained for the practice of occidental medicine and now converted to the traditional school, completed the distinguished group that accompanied us during our tour of the hospital and amiably replied to all our questions.

On our tour of the hospital we stopped in each department: general medicine; internal medicine; surgery; gynecology; pediatrics; ear, nose, and throat; eyes; acupuncture. The popularity of this hospital is indicated by the fact that an average of 400 consultations a day takes place there.

Traditional medicine excludes the operation as it is conceived in occidental practice. Acupuncture is employed even for appendicitis. But in a certain sense it is a kind of surgery and, as we have already mentioned, in extreme cases, when an operation of the occidental type is considered essential, it is performed with the consent of doctors of both medical schools.

We spent most of our time in the department where a heart patient was being treated. Traditional medicine is consistently successful in the treatment of cardio-circulatory disturbances. The problem of high blood pressure and arteriosclerosis receives special attention in this hospital. We noticed that in a patient's first examination his pulse is taken at much greater length than is customary in occidental practice and concluded that it must play a more important role in the diagnosis.

I was not there as a patient, but thanks to Dr. Chen Hsiaotsien's great courtesy, I was favored by having my pulse taken. The process lasted quite awhile and evidently left him satisfied. Other much more illustrious foreigners have been more than chance patients. When President Sukarno of Indonesia fell gravely ill toward the end of 1961, the Chinese government sent a medical team to Djakarta that treated him by means of traditional medicine and acupuncture. A prescribed kidney operation turned out to be unnecessary, and the President's health improved within a few weeks.

The Forbidden City

On this, our second visit to Peking, we of course revisited the Forbidden City, the walled enclosure containing the Imperial Palace. And so we again had the pleasure of walking through the palaces and seeing the marble terraces and the gardens with the artificial hills built by the fifteenth-century Emperor Yung Lo. On transferring his capital from Nanking to Peking the Emperor had tried to recreate on the banks of the Yangtze the landscape of his native region.

The original buildings of the Forbidden City have been restored several times following the fires and devastation which accompanied the struggles for control of the capital. Always the restorations have been faithful to the original design. The buildings are a monumental work from the point of view of architecture and decoration. They also reflect the unchanging dedication of the Chinese people to the principle of harmony uniting men and things.

Since our previous visit, an entire room of the Imperial Palace had been equipped for displaying the most priceless treasures unearthed from one of the 13 tombs of the Ming emperors. As is well known, ceramics was the great art of the Ming dynasty and these marvellous pieces from the tomb of one of its emperors reaffirm its excellence. When the day comes to open the other 12 tombs, China will possess a collection of ceramics rich enough to compensate in part—but only in part—for the treasure looted by international adventurers who visited the country disguised as explorers.

But the work must proceed very slowly because of the fragility of the treasure—extraordinary white and blue flower vases, blue enameled crowns encrusted with flowers, delicate ceramics placed between solid gold trays. What unparalleled riches a royal couple of that illustrious dynasty took with them under the earth when they passed from this world into history!

Crafts

Foreigners who wish to take home some souvenir of China buy it either in the antique shops or in the silk shops. Of the latter, one of the best is in the Chien Men section of Peking, behind the old station. The national art of weaving enjoys a centuries-old prestige. In ancient times the Greeks called China "Seres," that is, "the land of silk." Through national planning today, the textile industry has received an extraordinary impetus. We visited many textile factories in China from north to south, and some of them are among the most modern in the world. Since there was an urgent need to clothe the people after the long period of war and revolution, the number of spindles in cotton factories is today twice as great as before the Liberation. But the silk industry has not been neglected either, nor the wool and hemp industries.

In the antique shops the acquisition of really ancient pieces is limited by customs restrictions imposed to avoid a repetition of past abuses. Antiques can be purchased as long as they are not items which fall into the restricted categories. Such measures have contributed to the rebirth of the artisans, who today produce true works of art.

Our visit to Peking's Factory of Arts, which was organized in October of 1960, gave us the opportunity to see and talk to the skilled jade, ivory, enameled bronze, and coral craftsmen. This factory does not produce work for sale; it is primarily a factory-studio, and it also sends models to other factories. When we visited it, 25 elderly workers were teaching more than 650 artisans, of whom 35 percent were women. These masters of their crafts had a painful existence under the Kuomintang. "We worked hard for the rich, getting up very early and going to bed very late, and many times, when we didn't earn enough to live on, we had to sell paper or vegetables in the streets. It was the death of the crafts."

The Liberation is saving them—recruiting and organizing the craftsmen in cooperatives. One of the first was the enameled bronze cooperative. The craftsmen began to gather together and train young workers, until in the end they were working together in this factory. The crafts were thus rehabilitated; now they are beginning to pay and those working in them earn adequate wages.

A specialist in ivory carving showed us a beautiful piece of work which he had just finished and which had the look of ancient ivory. He labored for two years on another carving representing the Long March. It was made in one piece from a single elephant tusk. We saw pieces of carved ivory as much as 16 feet tall.

Despite their skill, however, some of these old craftsmen have learned to read only in the last few years; some now have such a passionate desire to read that they don't put their books down during the rest periods.

The renaissance of craft arts is accompanied by systematic work to re-establish the ancient production of ceramics. Today it is possible to see in a worker's home a plate or an amphora which in the past only a rich family could afford. It is not, of course, an original piece, but it is extraordinarily pleasing to the eye.

Ancient porcelain kilns such as the famous ones at Lung-chuan in Chekiang, which had been forgotten and abandoned, are again producing flower vases, teapots, lamps and all kinds of objects which are both useful and decorative.

3

NANKING AND WUHAN

In the lobby of our hotel in Nanking—a hotel that wasn't there in 1957—was a mural in vivid colors representing the popular movement "for iron and steel" in 1958. The results of this drive are very visible. After several days of visiting the new industrial, agricultural, and cultural establishments, I had a long conversation with the Vice Mayor of Nanking, Huang Chao-chun, an old friend of mine. He told me that between 1949, the year the new regime took power, and 1957, the total value of industry in Nanking had increased 14 times. Three years later, in 1960, this advance had doubled—despite the natural disasters occurring during those years. Industrial production in Nanking, he said, had increased from 700 million yuan (roughly 300 million U.S. dollars) in 1957 to three billion yuan (about $1.3 billion) in 1960.*

The variety of production had also increased considerably, with the chemical industry occupying third place after iron and steel. All sorts of things, from trucks to cameras, microscopes, and observatory equipment, are currently produced in Nanking. It would be tiresome to quote the detailed figures I gathered; suffice it to say that the objectives of the Second Five-Year Plan (1958-1962) were achieved and even surpassed in some areas a full year ahead of schedule—and this despite the droughts and floods which reached proportions during these years unknown since 1860.

A hundred years ago similar disasters took the lives of 10

---

* Because of the trade embargo between the United States and China, it is difficult to express Chinese money values in terms of U.S. dollars. At the time of the Chinese currency reform in 1955, the yuan was pegged at 2.343 to the dollar, and this is the figure I shall use throughout this book. But even assuming the accuracy of the figure in terms of foreign exchange, it does not necessarily reflect the yuan's internal purchasing power.

to 20 million people. Today they are faced and overcome with
relatively little loss of life. A European medical expert formerly
connected with the World Health Organization in Geneva assured me, after he had been in China for a month, that the
news published abroad about a state of widespread famine
was false.

Signs of Progress

Before beginning to visit the factories and the communes,
I took a turn around the city with Mr. Huang, and we also went
out to the suburbs so that he could show me the local road-
building program and the construction of apartment houses. One
may enter any building one chooses in the new housing developments and select at random the apartment one wishes to visit.
It is unlikely that hundreds of families could have been warned
ahead of time to clean their apartments and to dress for visitors.

These surprise visits are of particular value because they
show, frequently through some small detail, how the people's
standard of living is rising, little by little. It is hardly necessary
to say that we were always greeted cordially by the woman of
the house, often the grandmother who was there preparing the
meal while the rest of the family was working.

During my conversations with the Vice Mayor of Nanking,
I noted that, while he expressed satisfaction with what had been
accomplished, he also readily admitted the mistakes that were
made in the development of this or that project. I had noticed
this same quality in other Chinese authorities. In China, a visitor
to an important agricultural, industrial, or cultural enterprise
is urged to express his opinions and frankly. This is not just a
manifestation of traditional Chinese courtesy; it is an expression
of a desire to learn and to correct deficiencies.

They listened a little less carefully in 1961, however, than
they had in 1957, because with each year that passes their
technical cadres are more numerous and better prepared. But
you can still hear a factory manager, the director of a specialized
teaching institution, or the person in charge of an agricultural
exposition say that China is a technically backward country and
that they still have a great deal to learn.

Historical Background

Nanking was formerly a commercial city. Today it is a manufacturing center on the way to becoming one of the most important in the country. It already has more than 50 factories which employ an average of 1,000 workers each. Only enough of the ancient commerce is left as is necessary for the local economy. But with its decline, the corruption that manifested itself in waste and luxury has disappeared. Under the Kuomintang the richest people of that government preferred Nanking and made it a pleasure and vice center rivaling Shanghai. Gangsterism flourished unchecked, with a handful of reactionaries and crooks making money hand over fist. The city administration did not concern itself with raising either the standard of living or the cultural level of the population.

Today the city has 30 universities and other institutions of higher education, as compared to four before the Liberation, and several new theaters. In one of these theaters we saw a work which dealt with the famous nineteenth-century Taiping Rebellion. It reminded me of all that I had read concerning the epic struggle of the Chinese people to expel the Manchus from their soil.

The rebellion was born in Nanking, and though it had at first all the trappings of a first-class oriental intrigue, as it advanced it acquired a strong theoretical and political content. This has happened repeatedly throughout the history of China. Each time that a foreign power attempts to subjugate the nation by force, the entire populace reacts violently and with great cohesion to oust the invaders. Many such episodes in China's long history should serve as a warning to any madmen who today may be tempted to organize a "liberation in reverse" and impose again the rule of Chiang Kai-shek upon the Chinese people.

It was precisely the present "Lord of Formosa" who was the topic of conversation in the Mei Yuan Sin Chun Museum, which we had included in our Nanking itinerary. The museum contains maps and photographs of great interest and serves as a study center. It was here that the Chinese Communists and Chiang met in 1946.

Chiang Kai-shek used negotiations as a maneuver more than once. When Japan was defeated at the end of the Second World War, the Chinese people wanted to return to peaceful work. Chiang understood the necessity of making a gesture toward national reconciliation, and he invited Mao Tse-tung to go to Chungking for peace negotiations. He did it believing that Mao would not accept. But he miscalculated. Mao accepted the invitation and, eager to reach an agreement with the Kuomintang, he made several concessions, including the withdrawal of his forces from the liberated areas in Central and South China and reduction of his armed forces in proportion to the Kuomintang's reduction of theirs. This was the prologue to the Nanking negotiations.

In January of 1946 the cease-fire agreed upon as the result of those negotiations was ordered simultaneously by the Central Committee of the Communist Party and the Chiang Kai-shek government. But a month later the secret police of the Kuomintang burst into a Communist meeting, wounding some well-known militants. The fight began again.

The fake truce had served its purpose, and now Chiang concentrated on destroying the Communist forces. He was not successful—and so the United States began its famous mediation operation. General Marshall came to China and the China Aid Act, for the sole benefit of the Kuomintang, was introduced in the U.S. Congress. The American mediation had no other purpose than to neutralize, to paralyze, the Red Army.

Chiang, backed by the United States, suddenly felt himself to be strong militarily. But the U.S. aid to Chiang had been charging the atmosphere with anti-American feeling. An incident on Christmas Eve, when a drunken U.S. soldier tried to rape a student at the University of Peking, mobilized the students of the capital. The student protest extended to the rest of the country, taking the form of a general demand for the end of U.S. activities in China.

His mission having failed, Marshall returned to Washington. But, as the head of the museum told us: "We still maintained for quite a while that peace negotiations should be

renewed. However, on March 15, 1947, Chiang Kai-shek declared his determination to wage the civil war to the end. And
so he did. Two years later he had to go into exile on Formosa."

A Trip Across the Yangtze

A visit to the new chemical fertilizer plant and to other
factories still in the process of construction on the far side of the
river afforded us the very agreeable prospect of a motor-boat
trip on the Yangtze.

We love the Yangtze. In 1957 we sailed for days on this
great "river of golden sands" so closely linked with the history
of China and so beloved by its people.

Anyone who has seen the San Hsia or Three Throats of
the Yangtze will never forget them. Hsu Chih, a contemporary
writer, describes them exactly when he says that a trip through
them is like a voyage across an immense stage set with the
mountain and water scenery immortalized in ancient Chinese
paintings.

The mountains seemed almost about to strangle our boat
as it neared the Throats. At the very narrow passage between
the great peaks, the waters of the powerful river gathered into
themselves. It was like "a thousand seas poured into a cup," as
the great poet of the Sung dynasty, Su Tung-po, described this
spectacle of force and beauty.

Each of the Throats has given rise to a multitude of poems
and folk legends. One of the most popular has as its heroine
the goddess of the Wuhsia Throat. According to the legend, in
the third millenium B.C. the goddess came to aid Yu the Great,
who was organizing his people to do battle with the great waters
of the Yangtze. Before the flood season came, the goddess gave
him a beautiful book that contained all the information that was
necessary to control the waters. Aided by the goddess and the
young men of his court, Yu the Great managed to divide
the river.

The goddess also came to the aid of the people who were
threatened by the furious wild animals trapped when the waters
overflowed. She killed the tigers in the mountains and valleys
and sent celestial birds to guide boatmen over the shoals and

dangerous rapids. Finally the goddess and her maidens transformed themselves into the 12 peaks that extend their protection by night as well as by day to those who venture onto the river.

Our musings on such legends were interrupted by our arrival at the Chemical Fertilizer Corporation of Nanking. Organized in its present form in 1958, the Corporation began operations with a work force of 5,000 persons. Now it employs 18,000 and the plan for further development is only awaiting the construction of more buildings.

If, in certain branches of industry, the rate of production has had to be temporarily slowed down, that does not hold true for the fertilizer industry; for on its growth depends in great part the success of the Third Five-Year Plan (1963-1967) for agriculture.

At the time of our visit the Corporation consisted of eight units and was already one of the most important enterprises in East China. We were shown the graphs and drawings which traced the course of its growth. They were truly impressive; yet an engineer told us that still larger chemical fertilizer factories are planned for other parts of the country within a few years.

Before the Liberation the factory that we visited was just a small enterprise producing three different chemicals. Today it produces 42. In 1948 its annual ammonia production was 7,600 tons; in 1960, it was producing 750,000 tons—a 10-fold increase. With other products the story is the same. In 1948, 22,000 barrels of sulphur were produced; in 1960, 380,000 barrels. In 1948, 27,000 tons of chemical fertilizers were produced; in 1960, 465,000 tons. Taken as a whole, since it also produces potassium, phosphorus, and other agricultural materials, its annual production has increased 40 times since the Liberation.

We inquired about the conditions of the working men. We were told by the union representative in the plant that previously the workers had suffered a lack of food and clothing. Those who earned a low salary could barely subsist, while those who earned what was regarded as a large salary could buy more rice than the others, but that was all. All of them had a miserable life. "But now," he said, "there are some who earn as much as

117 yuan [about $50] a month, while the average wage is 68 yuan [about $30]."

These figures seem extremely low to a Westerner, but to evaluate what these wages mean it is necessary to see what one can buy with half a yuan in the canteen. Also bonuses for the best quality work and subsidies paid by the corporation (which are based to some extent on family circumstances) must be taken into account. Special subsidies are also paid to those who work in shops with high temperatures.

The old living quarters, very poor and unsanitary, have been largely replaced with blocks of houses which are simple but which conform to the recommendations of the Health Campaign. The amount of land devoted to housing has increased almost eight times since 1948, although the work force has increased by less than four times.

The Corporation maintains four elementary schools with 6,300 students, a secondary school, and an engineering school. It also runs a well-equipped and very large auditorium-theater where the cheapest ticket costs eight cents and the most expensive only twice that.

"This factory is important," its manager told us, "for several reasons. It is of Chinese design and all of its machinery is Chinese. It trains personnel, contributes to the formation of technical cadres, and in turn produces machinery for similar factories. Since the country needs fertilizers badly, the workers here are conscious of being engaged in a vital branch of production and they do what is expected of them. The initiative taken by the workers and their proposals to improve the work are gratifying. If a worker presents a useful idea to step up production he is rewarded. There are few work accidents because many precautions have been taken to avoid them. We have a station devoted to accident prevention."

We spent the whole day in the factory—a day that provided me with a great deal of valuable information on how the present Chinese economic policy is applied in practice. It also provided the basis of a lively discussion on our return trip across the Yangtze.

Wuhan

The first object of our attention in Wuhan was the new bridge over the Yangtze. This bridge joins two vast agricultural and industrial areas and, by opening the road from north to south, it has greatly stimulated the exchange of goods and raw materials. It took over two years to build because the problem of basing it firmly on the bottom of a river which is frequently turbulent and in flood was very complex. The bridge is over a mile long and has two levels, the upper one a highway and the lower one for a railway.

Soviet engineering experts contributed greatly to its construction. The characteristics of the Yangtze River presented the engineers with a series of difficulties which were resolved by the discovery of a method of construction that has already attracted many foreign engineers. Workers on special barges, using an enormous metallic framework, installed tubes of reinforced concrete almost five feet in diameter in the bottom of the river. As these tubes penetrated into the ground, others were inserted in such a way that they reached down to the bedrock, and were then filled with concrete. Thus, the builders managed to mount a ring of reinforced concrete columns.

We heard a sober description by the chief engineer of the extraordinary significance of the bridge in the national economy. Previously, trains had to be ferried over the river, and the residents of the three cities which straddle the banks of the Yangtze at this point (Wuchang, Hankow, and Hanyang—known collectively as Wuhan) had to cross in boats. Everything depended on the state of the river. A train took an average of two hours to be ferried across. Now it crosses in a minute. People are no longer delayed by bad weather.

"Quantity, quality, speed, harmony"—with these four words the man responsible for keeping the bridge functioning characterizes Wuhan's modern double-purpose bridge. He mentioned with an eloquent gesture of gratitude the Soviet engineers who directed its construction. And a Chinese engineer who was present added: "They were our teachers."

The Russians had pupils worthy of them; in Nanking I was told of the proposed construction in the near future of another bridge over the Yangtze, even longer than this one, which will be planned exclusively by Chinese engineers.

Boats pass under the Wuhan bridge in numbers that increase every year. The coastal passenger and cargo fleet has been enlarged, not only with new boats that come out of Chinese shipyards, but also with many salvaged from the bottom of the sea. "Nothing must be lost or wasted in China," is a comment that we heard frequently. And so the arduous task of raising sunken ships and cleaning up the rivers continues. One of the best boats that travels between Shanghai and Wuhan is the *Chiang Ya,* reclaimed by the Office of Salvage Engineering in Shanghai and modernized.

In 1956 it took nearly five months to lift the 4,000 tons of the *Chiang Ya,* but three years ago the *Kung Ping,* weighing 7,000 tons, was brought to the surface in 38 days.

Plans for developing the merchant marine look to the future, because as soon as the embargo is completely broken and all countries come to recognize China diplomatically, the industrial impetus which can be counted upon will expand foreign trade and create the need for a much larger merchant marine.

Visit to a Steel Complex

The visit to the Wuhan steel complex confirmed for me the impressive scale of the Great Leap Forward. When I attended the birth in 1957 of this great steel city, the second after Anshan, I could hardly comprehend the future envisaged for it. I had been astonished and somewhat skeptical on being shown the hills that were to be leveled to provide the widest possible area of expansion for blast furnaces and factories. But, viewing the site again in 1961, I saw that, indeed, the impossible had been accomplished. It was not difficult for me to believe the engineer who said that enough earth had been removed in making way for the Wuhan Steel Works to build a wall around the world one meter high by one meter wide.

The plant provides an impressive example of integral production—that is, production in which the various operations are linked. One can follow the process from the time the ore comes out of the mine to the moment the laminated sheets of steel are given the final inspection. In August, 1957, construction was begun on the first of the blast furnaces; it produced pig iron the following year and, the year after, steel. In 1960, production was extended to drawn steel (steel formed into specific shapes and sizes). In 1961 the steel works comprised seven mines, five coke ovens, two blast furnaces, a half dozen smaller furnaces and a dozen rolling mills. Since then, the plant has continued to grow.

The General Secretary of the Steel Works, Lin Wu, told us, nevertheless, that a decrease in the rate of production was beginning—a decrease anticipating the policy of "readjustment and consolidation" which was going to be applied on a wide scale throughout the country the following year (1962). "A temporary phenomenon," he explained. "It is a readjustment compensated for by an increase in variety and quality. In order to achieve better quality we have had to assure a proper balance within the productive process. In order to produce better quality steel we need first-class ore and coke."

This observation was corroborated by foreign experts who visited China that same year and who, judging by their statements in occidental professional journals, had been much impressed by the improvement in the quality of the steel beginning to be produced in China.

A few figures give one an idea of the activity of this company during the Great Leap Forward. In the first four months of operation the complex produced 150,000 tons of steel. By 1960 it was producing 740,000 tons a year. In regard to the development of the technical forces, there were 40,000 workers and office employees at the beginning; there were twice that number when I revisited the factory in 1961.

Lin Wu is one of those industrial managers characteristic of the Chinese "new industrial era"—a man so competent that in the United States or England he would certainly command a high managerial post. Speaking in the sober, precise fashion that characterizes those Chinese who are laying the foundations for the great economic thrust that is planned for the end of the Third Five-Year Plan in 1967, he explained the reasons for the startling progress of the Wuhan Steel Works:

(1) The adherence to the suggestions of the Communist Party and the application of the General Line for the building of socialism promulgated in 1958—a line that prescribed a clearly defined road for production. Then the workers and office employees themselves set the goal of constructing the steel mill at top speed, so eager were they to end poverty in China.

(2) The influence of the vanguard workers on the rest of the workers. In an effort of this kind an element of conviction, not compulsion, must be employed. It is indispensable for the masses to participate intimately in what they are doing, for them to know the vital importance of their work, and to realize fully the duty they have of doing it well. In this the action of the vanguard workers, stimulating and orienting the rest, is very important.

(3) A constant preoccupation with the worker's welfare, so that not only will he know he is working for the good of the whole Chinese people, but so that he will also be able to see in his own life the benefits of an improved economy. The life of the workers and office employees grows better every day.

(4) The application of the principle of "walking on two legs"—e.g., simultaneously *training* and *using* personnel and solving on the spot the difficulties encountered. For example, a cement problem arose. Instead of waiting until cement was sent in from outside, a cement factory was built within the company.

(5) The on-the-spot training of technicians. In the first phase of construction, 60 percent of all technicians were supplied by the Soviet Union. At present, 90 percent are trained in China, and most of them by the company itself. Personnel was reinforced last year by four new engineers and six draftsmen and technicians, all recruited from among the factory's own workers. The idea of a school for completing studies and for professional education during off hours was conceived at the time construction was begun on the factory.

Lin Wu concluded his explanation by telling us how, during the period of construction, the administration of the enterprise was strengthened by the participation of workers and office employees in management. He emphasized the practical results of that policy.

The "Three Cities"

During our stay in Wuhan we visited the three cities grouped there which are rivaling each other in an effort to renovate themselves. New avenues, large department stores, hundreds of modern housing units for workers can be seen in all of them.

At night, when we didn't go to the theater, we watched Chinese film documentaries in the Hsuan Kung Hotel dining room. These films, especially those in black and white, are excellent though rarely seen abroad. The color films we thought less successful, though they had certainly improved a great deal since our first visit.

The morning of the day we left we visited a pharmaceutical factory. Another of Wuhan's recently acquired claims to fame is that it is the chief source of drug supplies for central China. It has four modern factories that produce, among other things, antibiotics which previously had to be bought abroad. On the eve of the Liberation the country's few small laboratories manufactured hardly enough drugs to cover even the immediate needs of traditional medicine.

We also visited a nursery school, where a play was given in our honor. My wife and I immediately picked out a pair of future Peking Opera stars. The children were only five years old, but, as a matter of fact, they are not much older when they enter the preparatory academy of dance and pantomime. The photographs we took of these children are side by side in our album with those we took the following Sunday in Chang Tien, the main recreation spot of the city. This park is as delightful as an old Chinese embroidered silk cloth, with its field of lotus, its lake, and the mountains in the background.

We were in the airport waiting for our plane to Peking when a stir in the crowd warned us of the presence of some important personage. Presently, flanked by a couple of Chinese generals, appeared Field Marshal Montgomery, who had just arrived on the plane from Canton. He was wearing a red shirt and walking with a firm step, looking everywhere and certainly making comparisons, since it was also his second trip to the country. Later we saw him in Peking one night when he had dinner at the Hotel Peking where we were staying.

The visits of Viscount Montgomery have had the useful effect of making his compatriots think twice about swallowing whole certain reports on China that have appeared in British newspapers. Writing in the conservative *Sunday Times* of June 19, 1960, Montgomery said: "The system of People's Communes seems necessary for China; in fact, it is essential if the problems of any poor and backward nation are to be solved. . . . One hears it said that in the communes the children are separated from their parents. I investigated that point and found it to be entirely false."

Later, in his book, *Three Continents,* Montgomery developed in detail his argument for the recognition of "only one China," the Chinese People's Republic. He ridiculed the idea of "two Chinas," called American aid to the Formosa regime "mortally false." He also asserted Peking's right to occupy China's seat in the United Nations.

In the session of the United Nations Assembly of October 30, 1962, 42 nations voted in favor of the view taken by Viscount Montgomery. The United States still managed to get 56 votes, a smaller number than the year before, but enough to keep Chiang Kai-shek's fictitious "China" in the international organization while preventing any representation of 650 million Chinese. Twenty lamentable abstentions by countries that still move in Washington's orbit contributed to the continuance of a farce which harms the United Nations more than it does China. In 1963, on a vote to remove Chiang's "China" from the United Nations, 41 nations voted for the resolution, 57 against, and there were 12 abstentions.

4

SHANGHAI

One of the first scenes we saw in Shanghai was an argument between a policeman and a driver, a rare incident in China. A Chinese friend with us listened for awhile and then interpreted. It seems that the policeman, instead of handing the driver a summons, was giving him a lecture about the duties of citizenship in a socialist society. He made him understand that if everyone did as he pleased, the great China of today would not exist.

This educational effort, applied under the most diverse conditions, might move a Westerner to cynicism, but in great part it accounts for the decrease in crime and other offenses throughout China.

Occidental novels and movies, particularly American movies produced between the two World Wars, made Shanghai a symbol of oriental exoticism and adventure. Its night life, its cabarets in which big businessmen, native and foreign, vied for the favors of beautiful Chinese girls drawn to vice through hunger, its gambling houses, its opium smokers and free-flowing money all contributed to this image.

The reality of Shanghai's underworld prior to the Liberation went far beyond those superficial and lurid representations of the city's decay.

In 1957, looking for exact information about Shanghai's crime rate I went to Police Headquarters. There the method of operation of the four chief gangs who controlled Shanghai's underworld was explained to me. The names of the four crime czars who headed these gangs have not been forgotten in the city and their portraits hang in the Police Museum.

The activities of the four "big boys" were distributed thus: Huang Chen had the hotels, the bathing houses and the theaters under his jurisdiction. Tu Yueh-sen and his gang operated in the financial and commercial milieu, even controlling some of the main banks. Ku Tsu-shi and his group were in charge of the port and the traffic in drugs. Chen Tse-liang operated here and there with profit, but was not as powerful as the other three.

Their businesses flourished, particularly during the period of rapid disintegration of the Chiang Kai-shek regime. As occurs in all situations in a state of decay, the need for making as much as possible out of the circumstances encouraged illicit transactions and robberies. It was a contest to see who could steal most and fastest before the "good days" were over.

The crime organization utilized its profits to extend its operations. Full advantage was taken of all opportunities. Gang members managed to be included in the lists of those invited to weddings and birth celebrations. There they could either steal jewels and other objects of value or acquire intimate personal information that would enable them to set up full-fledged blackmail operations. Kidnappings of rich victims and the blackmail of wealthy persons who had committed an illegal act in some business deal or who had been involved in a secret love affair were commonplace. Operations were conducted at all levels of society and the profits included impressive sums taken from millionaires as well as pennies extorted from owners of pedicabs (little hand-drawn cars that took the place of taxis, and whose licenses were sold on the black market).

Prostitution was a particularly lucrative business for the gangsters, as it always is where dire poverty forces thousands of girls to make the bitter choice between slavery and starvation. The situation was so desperate among the poor that it was not unusual for parents to sell their little girls into this terrible servitude.

In all these operations the gangsters worked hand and glove with the police force. In many cases the police and the outlaws split the profits of criminal operations.

All this rottenness has been radically swept away under the present regime. The crime rate of Shanghai rapidly diminished in the first 10 years after the Liberation. It fell from 41,863 criminal cases in 1950 to 7,397 in 1956. And then a vertical decline followed until today there are not more than a dozen robberies a year. Political control and political policy of the police force are in the hands of trustworthy, capable individuals and the force has been completely pruned of its rotten elements.

Shanghai is no longer interesting for the writers of adventure novels. But its inhabitants prefer it that way.

Steel in Shanghai

From the window in our room at the Hotel of Peace in Shanghai, we could see the ferry boat, *Hupangpu,* transporting across the river the workers employed in the steel mills that are multiplying from year to year.

The metal workers of Shanghai evidently understand the value of what they have done and what they are going to do. Both the volume of production and its quality fill them with legitimate pride. As soon as we would enter a new factory the engineers would call our attention to certain types of laminated steel which could not have been made four years before, and to the seamless steel tubing. In the country as a whole, while the over-all rate of industrial production declined from 1961 to 1962, the production of superior quality steel rose by 52 percent.

In the Hsienfeng plant, manufacturing electric motors, the improvement in steel making has doubled production in comparison with 1957. It has also made possible the fabrication of a kind of electric motor which Chinese industry greatly needed.

In the parliamentary session of 1962, it was decided to concentrate the nation's resources on the development of agriculture during the next few years, in order to solve once and for all the problem of feeding the Chinese people. Since then, workers have competed with one another in their efforts to provide the machinery necessary for the modernization of the countryside.

The mural newspapers on the walls of many factories recall the struggle of the peasants to assure the industrial worker enough food to compensate for his efforts. Now it is the workers' turn to repay that debt, and they are sparing no effort in attempting to do so. Parts to repair agricultural machinery, from the most elementary to the most advanced, are manufactured by the tens of thousands. Aid to the peasants has become a question of honor for the industrial workers. I was told in Shanghai that the main metallurgical center of that city alone had sent four and a half million repair and replacement parts to the rural areas. The outside world can hardly realize what it means in China when the call goes out: "It is necessary to help the countryside." Millions and millions of men and women respond in a true popular mobilization that must be seen to be understood.

Shanghai, as well as Nanking, is aiding the development of agriculture in another way. The manufacture of chemical fertilizers has expanded greatly in the Shanghai area. Eleven new small factories making fertilizers and insecticides have gone into production. In fact, the farm chemicals industry is growing constantly all over China.

Minhang—Satellite City

Minhang, located about 20 miles outside of Shanghai, is one of the satellite cities through which Shanghai is solving the problem of overcrowding. One city is not enough? Then build another! This is the spirit in which the New China is tackling its difficulties.

There are several satellite cities around Shanghai, but we wanted to see Minhang because, in 1957, we had seen it when it was just a village surrounded by a wide expanse of uncultivated land. When we saw it this second time, it was a proud city of 70,000 inhabitants and was expected to grow still more.

The local authorities gladly took the trouble to show it off to us. The plans for construction, they said, had been carried out with few difficulties because everything was done from scratch and, hence, the freedom of initiative was very great. The city was first conceived as a small subsidiary of Shanghai's mechanical and electrical industry, but the original plan was broadened to include other industries. The chemical industry in Minhang is now second only to the steel industry.

The construction of factories was paralleled by the building of workers' homes, which were placed in such a way that they would be close to the factories but protected from smoke, noise and crowding. Each unit has four or five stories and the apartments contain two or three rooms plus kitchen, bathroom, and balcony.

Eleven public buildings were put up along the main street in less than 80 days, including the hotel where we stayed. The other buildings were stores, schools, offices, and, at the end of the street, almost in the country, a hospital with 340 beds.

Complete generator units, boilers, turbines of up to 100,000 kilowatts, electric machinery and ball bearings are among the important products now coming off the production lines of Minhang. We saw its machine tool equipment displayed at the Shanghai Industrial Exposition the day after we visited the satellite city. (According to the European Committee for Co-operation of Machine Tool Industries, the machine tool industry in China in 1962 was ahead of that of the United States. A study made by that committee fixed at 75,000 the number of Chinese machine tools produced in 1960, as compared to the U.S. production of 34,000.)

The Industrial Exposition

Our visit to the Shanghai Industrial Exposition allowed us to get a clear picture of the present state of industrialization in China. It also gave us an idea of what Chinese industry will be like in the years ahead. On the basis of what is produced today, and with the explanations provided by the two experts who accompanied us, we could discern the rising curve of an industrial sector which is only waiting for agriculture to catch up with it before realizing its full potential.

Shanghai's Industrial Exposition is continuous; that is, if in a given month Shanghai's industry has produced something worthy of being shown there, it is incorporated into the material already on display. When we saw it, its principal pavilions were dedicated to the electrical, the metallurgical, the chemical, the textile, and light industries. We saw the latest model of a machine that provides by itself all of Shanghai's lighting, a precision machine for perforating earth to facilitate its removal, and an aviation instrument which, according to one of our guides, the Americans did not believe the Chinese would be able to make without their help.

From examining wool-spinning machines, pharmaceutical products, and photography equipment we turned to the impressive dais, the center of attention of a group of school children, where models of the Phoenix automobile were on display. A model boat exhibit was also receiving a lot of attention. A showcase full of toys attracted both adults and children; the imagination and the artistic sense of the Chinese combine to fabricate delightful playthings. A large number of graphs and charts showing how industry helps agriculture were also on display.

Decentralization of Industry

In order to include each region of China in the advance of the nation as a whole, a policy of industrial decentralization had been instituted by the government. China is an enormous country. To measure the effort which has been made in the last 15 years, it is necessary to look, not only at the major cities like Shanghai, but also at the more remote regions. Take the example of Inner Mongolia, the first Chinese autonomous region. Here, before the Liberation, a population of 11 million lived in an area greater than France, Germany, and Italy combined. It was a pastoral population, culturally backward beyond all description, to whom industry was practically unknown.

Within two decades the economic and cultural profile of Inner Mongolia has changed fundamentally. Industrial production has increased 25 times. The blast furnaces of its new steel industry have turned out hundreds of thousands of tons of steel. In fact, in this short time, the city of Paotow has acquired international fame for its steel production.

In the area of education, there was not a single secondary institution in the whole region. Today it has 10 secondary schools, and the number of schools in general has multiplied seven times.

Light Industry

The redistribution of agricultural and industrial production carried out according to the official plan is helping the development of raw materials and consequently of light industry. Formerly light industry was located mainly along the coast since this was in the interests of the foreign exploiters who more or less controlled the ports and who brought in the required raw materials.

Today the coastal area receives only as much agricultural and industrial support as it needs from the point of view of the national interest. By preference the new factories are being built near the source of their raw materials. The regions in central China where cotton flourishes have been favored for the construction of textile factories. Sugar refineries are to be found in the Northeast, where the sugar crops are grown.

Light industry has come to occupy one of the first places in China's national economy. Products that previously were almost all imported are now produced in Chinese factories in quantities which meet a large part of the domestic demand. These products include radios, watches (Chinese watch production has begun to alarm Swiss exporters), bicycles (an important means of transportation in China), cameras, fountain pens (the pen I always carry with me was made in Shanghai and writes beautifully), optical products, plastic articles of many kinds, perfumes, shoes, and various household items.

An official report put out at the end of 1962 mentions 750 different products produced on an experimental basis by light industry in the three main centers—Shanghai, Peking, and Tientsin. Of these, more than 100 were chosen to be mass-produced. Their quality in design and operation has already improved greatly. By 1965 the production of light industry will be three times that prior to the Liberation.

The plan of geographic redistribution, which has led to the establishment of light industry in the territories of the national minorities, has had the happy effect of introducing a great variety in the design and color of the articles produced.

The profusion of silk covers, woolen articles, tableware, etc. that is offered for sale in a large department store such as the one we visited in Shanghai illustrates the quality and variety of the products of Chinese light industry. This profusion also illustrates the improvement in the living standards of the Chinese people. Most of them would never have thought of entering one of these stores 15 years ago—partly because they had no money to spend on anything except food, and partly because, even if they had the money, there was little to attract their interest.

Communications

Shanghai is one of the centers of a vast network of expanding communications. The vastness of the country makes the problem of internal communication one of capital importance.

Exactly 40 years ago there were, in all of China, only about 750 miles of modern highways. In the first 10 years of the Revolution, almost 200,000 miles of new highways were constructed. One of the most ambitious projects was the construction of the Sikang-Tibet highway, which stretches over 1,200 miles and crosses rivers, frozen surfaces, virgin forests, and mountains as high as 13,000 feet, previously almost impassable.

The exchange of goods has been greatly increased as a result of the improved transportation system and new human communities have been born. Gormo, a place on the Tibetan highway formerly inhabited only by wild animals, is now a small city of 30,000 persons. With the building of new roads, bridge construction has also developed. The favorite style here has always been the bridge with stone arches, and this is the kind which is being built now, in conformity with the people's taste.

The Port

The port of Shanghai consists of six main docks and two others for smaller ships. The fifth dock is the one which receives the ships of the Chinese coastal service. Its director, Wan Chenshui, told me about the life of a longshoreman under the old regime.

Brutalized by work fit only for beasts of burden, the longshoremen slept on the docks, on the pavement, or in nearby streets, sometimes because they had no time to go to their shacks in a slum on the opposite side of the city, sometimes because they lacked the energy to do so. Their wages hardly allowed them to buy enough rice to live on. And we won't even speak of medical attention, workers' insurance, or pensions. When the workers were no longer able to carry loads and had become sacks of skin and bones, they were thrown out on the garbage heap and had to beg for a living.

In the New China the longshoreman has been lifted to the level of a human being. Machinery spares him the hardest part of dock labor; his wages provide him with a decent living, and he has a Sailors' Club. Wan Chen-shui says he "has no patience" with those outside of China who are writing about today's situation. (His contact with foreign sailors keeps him in touch with what is written abroad.) "They don't understand anything," he said to me. "They don't even know how to look back in order to compare. I'd like to have seen some of those newspapermen working on this dock as longshoremen 15 years ago."

His brief angry digression rapidly gave way to an interesting account of the progress which had been made in the port since I saw it in 1957. Then, ships from only 12 to 16 nations arrived at Shanghai. By 1961 ships from close to 30 nations docked there. The movement of foreign ships had doubled. But still more encouraging was the greater variety of merchandise ready for export.

I noted some categories of export and import. Among the former were cereals, rice, beans, canned meat and fish, fruit, silk and velvet and some cotton fabrics, machinery (particularly textile machinery), hemp, leather, furs, green and red tea. Imports included chemical products (principally fertilizers), special metals, sugar, rubber, and synthetic cotton.

The general campaign for technical renovation has been received with great enthusiasm by the port workers. As we traveled along the dock in Mr. Wan's automobile he pointed out various results of the campaign. Not only have new machines come to take over more and more of the work of loading and unloading, but also the workers have found ways to shorten the time these operations take and to increase precautions in transporting and storing the merchandise.

The manufacture of cranes in China had ended the need to import them all from abroad at great expense. In 1958 eight cranes were in use on the docks; now there are 22. The largest are still imported but the five-ton cranes were made in Shanghai.

"We have established a small basis for advanced dock work," the director finished by telling us, "but we still have much to do."

Health Program

Shanghai is one of the cities which has carried the Health Campaign ahead most energetically. The statistics on the results of this campaign throughout the country and an estimate of its merits by international medical authorities who have visited China are to be found in reports made public by part of the occidental press. On our second visit, as on our first, we met foreign doctors of high repute in their own countries who in general were much impressed by what they had seen in China. Specialized English publications such as the *British Medical Journal, The Lancet,* and *The New Scientist* have mentioned among other things:

(1) The fact that China had freed itself completely from cholera as of 1949 and from smallpox as of 1950.

(2) The successful struggle against gastrointestinal illnesses in areas where typhoid fever, amoebic dysentery, and similar infections previously claimed many victims.

(3) The fact that in only eight years 860 new hospitals have been built—an average of about two a week.

(4) The role in sanitation of the street committees, which do not leave it to the quarterly hygienic-medical inspections to make sure that the Health Campaign's directives are carried out, but look after it constantly themselves.

Even in the slums, the primitive sections that have not yet been replaced maintain a level of cleanliness unknown previously even in neighborhoods where higher social classes lived. Street cleaning is almost an obsession, each person being expected to clean the area in front of his house. Aside from the penalty that is imposed, those who neglect this task acquire a bad reputation among their neighbors.

In the conference of specialists on venereal diseases held at Peking in 1960, not more than 30 cases of syphilis were reported from eight Chinese cities, including Peking, Shanghai, Tientsin and Canton. Today new cases are extremely rare.

Social Legislation

In one of the Shanghai factories I had the opportunity to talk to a union representative about the application of social legislation.

Labor insurance is required in China in all enterprises that employ as many as 100 laborers and office employees. All workers, regardless of sex or nationality, benefit from this insurance. A laborer or office employee who falls ill for a period of up to six months receives, in addition to free medical attention, from 60 to 100 percent of his salary, according to the number of years he has worked. After six months he receives from 40 to 60 percent of his salary.

The funds applied to labor insurance are the sole responsibility of the enterprise and are administered by the management and the union.

The employee who is sick is taken care of in the company's hospital or clinic but, if he needs extra attention that the company cannot provide, he is sent to a specialist or a clinic.

Labor insurance also covers preventive medicine. The personnel of factories, businesses, public administrations, and schools receive the benefit of a free medical and X-ray examination once a year. Thus, certain illnesses are often caught in time to be halted or cured.

This preventive medical care goes hand in hand with the use of sanitariums, rest homes, and night clinics, distributed all over the country and maintained at the expense of the unions. The night clinics are an institution which is as original as it is practical. They allow workers suffering from a chronic condition which is not critical to receive treatment without having to interrupt their regular work.

As for the famous beaches, monopolized in the past by a rich native and foreign clientele, they are today recreation spots for the workers—a health benefit of untold value.

5

ANHWEI PROVINCE

We had intended to revisit beautiful Hangchow, a city which justifies the proverb, "Paradise in heaven, and Hangchow on earth." However, we did not regret the rough journey we took instead through the province of Anhwei, one of the poorest provinces of the pre-revolutionary period and hence one of the best for comparative purposes.

Talking with the local authorities I soon assembled background information about Hofei, the capital of the province and a city with more than 2,000 years of history behind it. It is situated between the Yangtze and the Hwai Rivers, which gives it special importance from the point of view of hydraulic policy. But, aside from this, its development in the space of 13 years makes it one of the best places to form a picture of what has been accomplished under the Revolution.

In this short period of time, the population has risen from 50,000 to 550,000. That, as we have seen, is not a rare phenomenon in China. But few other places in the country show so radical a change in living and working conditions.

Hofei used to be a sleepy small town; indeed, it was hardly more than a big village, poorly designed, dirty, and forgotten. There was not a bit of industry, only artisans producing handmade articles. Chinese hands suffice in themselves to produce beauty, as we could see in the few pieces of old furniture in the hotel that survived the efforts to modernize it.

Today new factories rise on the land that once held the artisans' workshops. The local planner who accompanied us gave us the figures: 272 factories, large and small, employing in all more than 100,000 workers. In other words, there are twice as many workers in Hofei today as there were people before the Liberation.

"The structural reforms," we were told, "have been made

while keeping in mind that the agrarian revolution now under-
way is going to require an even wider expansion of industry."
The main drive was made in 1958, the year the Great Leap
Forward was instituted. Then the city really "moved ahead with
industrialization," with steel as the key link. From that time until
now 300 smelting furnaces have been installed, each with a
capacity of almost nine cubic yards, plus ten converters of 300
tons each, and another 300 small converters of a half ton each.
Today Hofei produces 100,000 tons of pig iron and 17,000
tons of steel a year, and its working population includes 20,000
trained metallurgical workers.

More than statistics, it is the comments of the older people
who have witnessed this transformation—"almost without believing it," as the old head of one small workshop of other days
put it—that give a true idea of the dimensions of the city's
modernization.

Along with heavy industry, light industry has also been
developed. A comparison of the over-all value of industry in
1960 with that of 1949 shows that it has increased more than
300 times.

It is mainly in construction that the change borders on the
unbelievable. The village of yesterday, with its three miles of
urban surface, has today become a city covering an area of 30
square miles. Entirely new streets reach out in all directions.
We walked down what used to be the main street, where people
always strolled on Sundays. It was a mud road broken by partial
attempts at paving. It won't be there long because the people
who still live in the homes that line it will be moving into new
housing as soon as a few more already planned blocks of housing
are finished.

The passenger bus was an unknown luxury in the Hofei of
15 years ago. Today the city has nine bus lines, certainly insufficient for a population which has increased by 10 times, but
providing, nonetheless, the basis for a transportation system
which will replace the bicycle for getting the workers to the
factories.

There are 4,000 automatic telephones in Hofei today and
the city can now be reached by rail. Before, the only way to

reach Hofei was by road. Air and water transport service are also available. The city's isolation has been broken down to open the way for a wide commercial and cultural exchange.

In the too-recent past Hofei, though a provincial capital, had only one second-class school. That was all. Today there are 193 primary and secondary schools, with 8,924 teachers and professors and 95,000 students.

Theatrical activity was centered before in a single theater that was only a hut. Today there are 10 theaters and movie houses with a total capacity of 9,000 seats. And two more are being built in the new workers' housing projects.

Before, there was one hospital worthy of the name, with 30 beds. Today the city has 316 public health institutions, 20 of them hospitals with a total of 4,890 beds.

But the pride of the city is its polytechnic institute—the Industrial University of Hofei, a great center for the training of technicians. These men and women, after receiving their degrees and acquiring practical experience in the factories of the province, are sent to all corners of China, including Shanghai, to carry out the tasks that have been projected in the Third Five-Year Plan.

The present University was just a small institute, like many others before the Liberation, with only one specialty. Since then it has become the industrial institute for the carboniferous zone to the south of the River Hwai. It still has limited goals. But the pressing demand for technicians created by the development of heavy industry required the creation of new schools, and this, in turn, required a large group of capable university professors. The director gave us the figures as we walked through the impressive building: before the Liberation, 200 students and 30 teachers; today, 4,500 students and 700 professors working in six great schools—geological exploration, chemical engineering, radio engineering, mechanical-electronic engineering, architectural engineering, and general technological training. In Chinese planning the study of architecture, engineering, and economics is tightly linked.

Following the principle of combining theoretical and practical work, the students of Hofei University go down into the mines to extract coal one day, and go to the blast furnaces "to take out the melt" on another. Every year the students spend eight to eight and a half months studying and experimenting in one of the University's 38 laboratories, a month to six weeks in productive labor, and two months on vacation.

The field of scientific research is being rapidly expanded all over China. At the Industrial University of Hofei a research program includes: (1) subjects assigned by the central government; (2) subjects prepared by the local People's Committee; (3) subjects proposed by the various ministries concerned with industry; and (4) subjects chosen by the University itself.

In this way, while scientific research serves the country's general planning, it also takes into account the immediate regional needs and does not limit itself to the purely theoretical. One of my companions made the observation: "It is the proletarianization of education."

As they finish their professional training the more advanced students at the Industrial University of Hofei cooperate on a project in which the government is much interested—the search for natural resources and economic potentialities that will contribute to making China a leading industrial nation. This task is being carried out under a plan formulated by the various economic ministries and the Academy of Sciences. Expeditions today are combing the country. For more than a year a team of agronomists has been studying the possibility of developing agriculture and cattle-raising in Tibet. The most appropriate lands are used for experimental crops, in order to establish which will give the largest yield.

The deserts of Inner Mongolia are being studied by another group of scientists who have discovered places where cotton can be grown with greater success than had ever been thought possible in so arid a region.

The expedition that was sent to the southeast coast reported optimistically on the utilization of great stretches of land, never before cultivated, for the production of coffee, maguey, and other tropical crops.

Another scientific group, made up of 300 members, has carried out exhaustive research in Szechwan and Yunnan, finding in the latter province many trees and herbs that can be used in the medical and food industries and for the manufacture of fibers and dyes.

Taken together, these projects indicate that science has been mobilized to serve the economy. And those who are directing that mobilization are sure that China still has immense resources, the exploitation of which will compensate for deficiencies resulting from the nation's long-standing technical backwardness.

The Mountain of Mei

We left Hofei in an automobile for the town of Mei Shan. (Shan means mountain in Chinese.) Before our departure a young woman doctor surprised us with a visit at the hotel. She wanted to take my blood pressure as a precaution on account of the altitude.

It is extremely interesting to visit the mountain regions in which, in many cases, agriculture has started from zero. First comes the reclamation of the land or the watersheds formerly considered entirely useless because of the altitude, temperature, and humidity. After a couple of years' work they have been transformed into cultivated areas producing wheat (better with each harvest), rice, and a variety of other crops.

The nearby forest provides abundant bamboo for the construction of farmers' houses of superior quality. Mechanization was impelled by the necessity of transporting the wood from the forests, and with it has come the opening of local roads and finally real highways. The car in which we rode rarely hit a bump.

After awhile we stopped at the first hydraulic project of the province in the valley of the formidable River Hwai. In earlier days, when the water rose, flooding and the loss of crops were inevitable. Then Chairman Mao gave the call: "Control the River Hwai!" and adequate dams were built here at a rapid rate. The People's Communes and the state participated jointly in the task. The communes ceded some of their lands for the project and provided labor in a degree compatible with the priority given to their own agricultural needs. They were the first to benefit from the new projects and they benefited in two ways: by securing irrigation waters for their crops and electrical power for their homes and farms. Villages that had never previously known electric lights have them today.

The state cooperated by providing the money necessary to employ supplementary labor and by supplying construction materials.

The whole project was planned so that the greatest possible advantages could be obtained from the effort expended. Hence, the project will contain the floods, provide irrigation and electrical energy to a wide area, and stimulate the development of internal traffic. Some of the largest canals built to serve the latter purpose are as much as 75 yards wide and 16 feet deep; they permit the passage of 1,000- to 2,000-ton ships.

The project has already valiantly survived two years of drought. During the lunch that interrupted our trip and introduced us to several delightful examples of Chinese rural cooking, the conversation revolved around plans to end the area's vulnerability to natural disasters. The system proposed would, it was agreed, require five years more before it could be counted upon to stop the serious damage caused by floods and droughts.

This town, despite the hydraulic works and the communes, gave the impression of being lost in the mountains. But the authorities approached the great national questions with sharp perception. Noting this quality on the part of local leaders, the British labor deputy, R. H. S. Crossman, has written: "What has impressed me most in China is that Mao Tse-tung has succeeded in creating, in a relatively brief period of time, a team of local leaders who are very dedicated to their work and who do not wait for decisions to come from higher administrative centers before they act." Later on, in the same report, he observed: "Whatever may be the past errors of the Chinese Communists, I believe that they will be a good deal more successful than the Soviets in modernizing their agriculture. And for a very simple reason. The Russian Revolution was exported from the city to the country. The Chinese Revolution began as a peasant revolution and only entered the cities after taking power." And he went on to make a further judgement: "With the discipline characteristic of this people and a solid central power, they will finally succeed in making China the most powerful nation in the world."

As we advanced toward Mei Shan the landscape began to resemble certain rugged parts of Switzerland. A splendid sunset softened the rough landscape when we drove into a town that was apparently just beginning to be built. And, in effect, the old village had to be abandoned to make way for the impressive dam that rose before us. We were going to visit it the following day.

The hotel seemed encrusted on a mountain peak. Small but very snug and agreeable, it was built mainly for the dam engineers and occasional outside visitors. It was run by some Chinese girls, two of whom could well have appeared on the cover of one of those illustrated magazines printed in Peking to be sent abroad.

They had kindly installed a radio in our room and by chance the first thing I heard when I turned it on was *The Voice of America* attacking the Peking government on the occasion of a debate about China's membership in the United Nations. When I mentioned this the next day, the only reaction was: "Could you hear it well?" (The Chinese do not jam broadcasts from outside.)

After supper we talked with the engineers from the dam. The conversation was very general—and very free. Detailed explanations were kept for our visit to the site. We were struck by the spontaneity with which they emphasized how much Chinese engineers have still to learn from other countries. (This is something that I began to doubt the next morning on visiting the dam, for it is the highest multiple-arch dam in the world.)

A couple of representatives of the peasants' organizations joined our after-dinner discussion group. The disaster of 1954 was mentioned. "Without this dam," they told us, "it would have been even worse this year."

There are 60 People's Communes in the district, and among their members are some elders who recall what happened in 1896: "The worst disaster in a thousand years. It is not known how many died as a consequence of the fury of the River Hwai." The most direct picture of what the floods were like that year is conveyed in a few words and a line drawn by one of the terrified residents who had fled to the highest rock he could find.

"The water came up to here," he wrote, thus summing up the millenary tragedy of the Chinese peasantry, that only ended when the present regime embarked upon its large-scale agrarian policy.

The visit to the dam proved to be worth the long trip from Hofei. It is an audacious construction, a formidable breach in the mountains 20 feet thick and 82 feet long. In the process of building, the gap that was to hold the complete construction was blocked off by two mud dams, one on each side, so that work could continue with the least possible risk of new floods by the Hwai.

A completely Chinese achievement in its execution, this challenge to nature rose stone on stone, until the "multiple-arched dam of Mei Shan" was finished—just 26 months after construction was begun.

The water from the lake behind the dam passes through four turbine generators, each with a capacity of 10,000 kilowatts. The spillway has seven floodgates and can drain off 11,000 cubic yards of water per second. One of the engineers who was guiding us commented: "Even an 'explosion' of water such as the one we were talking about last night, the one in 1896, could not do any harm at all today."

During a halt in the tour, the head agronomist of Mei Shan enumerated for us the advantages of the dam: (1) flood prevention; (2) irrigation; (3) cheaper electricity as well as a supply adequate to cover the large deficit that existed; (4) navigation; (5) fishing. (Fish weighing up to 30 pounds are plentiful, a great aid in feeding the people.)

The irrigation projects on the Mountain of Mei, as in the rest of China, have been developed with indisputable efficiency and their benefits will be felt to an even greater extent in the coming years. But, as with everything in this land of self-criticism, the hydraulic policy is submitted to constant examination in order to find out how it can be improved; what the occasional errors are due to; why a project that was well conceived on paper does not turn out in practice as expected. Thus in various provinces projects have been revised because they would have wasted too much water, or because they would have made previously fertile land too alkaline.

This means that whoever wants to emphasize the weak side of Chinese planning will find plenty of specific examples to support his position. Not only that, but he will not have to go far to find them; they can be encountered in reports in the Chinese press. But the person who wants to get to the bottom of things will realize that a relatively few mistakes in the development of the great irrigation policy are not significant.

The chief engineer at the Mei Shan dam explained that in certain areas the effectiveness of what he called "the Great Hydraulic Revolution" has been proven with a speed that has surprised even the technicians themselves. "But," he added, "you can't solve with one Five-Year Plan or with two a problem that has been plaguing Chinese agriculture for centuries."

A Talk with Some Veterans

The trip to Mei Shan held a surprise for me. On our second day there we learned of a rest home in the vicinity for veterans of the revolutionary struggles.

Having carefully studied the exhibits in the Military Museum of the Revolution in Peking and in other museums, and having heard from the lips of officers how the powerful army of today was formed, we wanted to get from the protagonists themselves the story of their experiences during the fighting and the famous Long March.

The setting could not have been more typically Chinese. The rest home, with its gardens and orchards, dominates a valley that was still in bloom at the end of summer. We were served tea with delicious local sweets, including sugared chestnuts such as we had never eaten before. Of the three veterans who took the lead in answering our questions, one of them, Chan King-an, had distinguished himself in the guerrilla actions that led to the formation of the initial units of the Red Army. The other two, Liu Teng and Li Teh-tsun, had taken part in the Long March. Now they lived here with their families in retirement, on pensions, although they were not inactive. They declared themselves ready, in spite of their age, to return to battle if the independence of China should be threatened. They follow closely the activities of the government, the work in the communes

of the region, the hydraulic operations. They even keep an eye
on events abroad, to judge by the questions they asked me—some
of them about the struggle the Spanish people are waging today
against Franco.

Chan King-an was the first to tell his story. "After 1932,"
he told us, "the main part of the Revolutionary Army dispersed
under orders, distributing itself in conveniently selected places
to avoid being crushed by an enemy force numerically far
superior to our own. The 28th Army had only 2,000 men. The
Kuomintang had six well-equipped divisions.

"But we fought hard for three years. If the enemy had an
overwhelming numerical advantage on their side, we had on ours
an enthusiasm that they lacked—that, and our revolutionary
inventiveness. Sometimes we attacked the enemy from behind,
other times in front, always disconcerting him, so that the
Kuomintang did not know where we were nor how strong
we were.

"Our morale," said Chan King-an in a very firm voice,
"was perhaps our greatest asset. No one knows the value of a
handful of men ready for anything, who do not say to themselves, 'It is madness to try that!' but who instead try it and
succeed.

"At the same time we knew how to be prudent. We didn't
engage in battles that could cause us irreplaceable losses and
cripple our fighting organization for a long time. Skill and
flexibility were the Communist policy, an exact political line laid
down by Comrade Mao.

"Tight liaison existed between our army and the masses,
and equality prevailed among ourselves. Strong discipline was
enforced, and no looting or abuses committed by force were
permitted. We were aided by the people, who advised us of
every enemy move. It was a hard and exhausting life, but we
bore it cheerfully. We were sure that we would triumph.

"Our losses were offset by the enlistment of volunteers. The
Kuomintang tried to bribe the peasants so that they would inform
on us. They offered them the following rewards: five yuan for a
corporal handed over to them tied hand and foot; 30 yuan for
an officer; 1,000 yuan for the head of a regiment or a division;

10,000 yuan for the head of an army corps. But in the end they were the ones who were tied up, and by us."

Mao Tse-tung's name was mentioned frequently in the course of the conversation and often I was reminded of the stories told about that great leader in the book, *On the Long March with Chairman Mao*, written by Chen Chang-feng, the man who was his orderly. A direct and deeply human account of the founder of the New China is given in this book.

"Comrade Mao's life," wrote Chen, "was very simple and I rapidly became accustomed to his habits. His only baggage consisted of two blankets, a cloth sheet, two gray uniforms like those the soldiers wore, a wool vest, an old mended umbrella, a little bowl, and a bag with nine compartments. He carried his maps, documents and books in the bag."

From time to time Chen received a scolding. "Chen Chang-feng, what happened to the rice I put aside last night? After all the sufferings the peasants endure to gather a handful of rice! You surely didn't throw it away!"

One day Mao asked him: "Don't you want to write home?" "Chairman, I'd like to, but. . . ." "But you still don't know how to write, isn't that it? Very well, come here. I'll write the letter for you."

During the first stage of the Long March, Chairman Mao lived with another comrade in an old abandoned temple on a hill. He had to walk a long distance every day to attend the Military Committee's meetings, and at night he still had to write reports which kept him working until the early morning hours. His health began to suffer. Chen wanted to find a good doctor who would be Mao's personal physician. "No," answered the Chairman, "when there is such a scarcity of doctors in the army, how can I monopolize one?" But he accepted a male nurse who would "come in when he was called" and who knew how to take his temperature and give him injections. "My health isn't so bad, after all, and a nurse is all I need."

After the battle at the Tatu River in June of 1935, the army of the Long March reached the foot of a tall mountain covered with snow, Chia-chinshan. It was the first time that Mao's troops had faced the test of so painful an ascent. Chen tells how the Chairman encouraged everyone. At one point he held up his orderly in his arms. At the summit, "with his feet sunk deeply in the snow, the Chairman turned around to follow the movements of those comrades who had not yet reached the peak." There was no hardship that Mao Tse-tung did not share with his men, as just another plain soldier.

Then came the advance over the steppes. The food supply diminished with each day that passed. One day Chen and his comrades cooked the leather used to make soles for their shoes. They were having a small banquet when the Chairman approached the group. "What are you eating?" he asked. "Pork," someone answered. "Where did you get it? Did you break discipline?" Mao demanded. He did not tolerate acts of pillage, no matter how small they might be, for the bad impression of the Red Army such acts would leave among the peasants. Finally they told him the truth. "Well, if you can eat it, I can too." And he helped himself to a slice.

In September of 1935, after conquering the snow-covered mountains and the steppes of Sikang and Szechwan, the Red Army units continued their irresistible advance to Kansu. The Long March was approaching its end. The Chairman's face shone and he was heard to exclaim with enthusiasm: "We have already crossed ten provinces. On the other side of this mountain we will enter the eleventh, Shensi. There we have our base; there we shall be in our home!"

Farewell to Anhwei

On the way back to Peking we made one more stop—in the city of Pengpu, located four hours by railway from Hofei. Pengpu is one of the ancient little cities of the interior which foreigners rarely see. But it would be a mistake to think of Pengpu as being backward and forgotten. Since the Liberation its population has tripled; large numbers of workers, engineers and technicians have come here to work, for this is one of the strategic points in the provincial hydraulic system, of which the Mei Shan dam is the apex.

As we crossed the wide plateau through which the canals had been built, the principal official of the town explained the efforts which had been made to interest the country people in raising cattle. That evening, in the hotel lounge, we saw a short movie dedicated to a glorification of the communes and developed in a genre that was something between operetta and ballet. Farm animals were the chief characters and we decided that the little pigs and the ducks were the most charming.

After the movie we had time, before catching the Shanghai-Peking Express, to rest a few hours in a large, comfortable hotel room typical of the interior. It had been modernized since the Liberation but still retained some of the atmosphere of old China. Everywhere we traveled in the provinces, as well as in the major cities, we found the hotels comfortable and the service excellent. The Shanghai Express was comfortable, too, but we weren't too happy about having to catch it in the middle of the night.

6

THE PEOPLE'S COMMUNES

"It is frightening how these people work!" exclaimed an English visitor to China to me at one point during my travels.

He was right. If there is a people who have known centuries of hard labor, it is the Chinese, especially the peasants. For some foreign visitors the symbol of that labor is the bamboo pole that permits the bearer to carry unbelievable burdens on his shoulders. But the bamboo pole, which performed such great services during the first years of national construction when means of transportation were scarce, still does not give a true picture of the harshness of life in the countryside and in the ports, in the textile factories of Shanghai and in the mines of Chungking or old Manchuria, prior to the proclamation of the People's Republic.

Until the Revolution the plight of the Chinese peasant epitomized the social history of the country. There were, it is true, periods of relief in his existence that coincided with the appearance of reforming emperors or with the transitory triumph of scholars of a progressive spirit. But from very ancient times the owners of the large estates had, bit by bit, absorbed the holdings of the small landowners until their successors became lords of both lands and people, combining in their persons the despotic master and the usurious money lender.

In the long periods of famine, poor peasants sold the last piece of land they had left and then sold themselves, or their children, strengthening in this way the reign of slavery. This happened not only in the feudal period, but up to the very eve of the Revolution. It ended forever in 1949.

With this historical background in our minds, we began to tour the People's Communes, the Chinese innovation in the realm of agrarian policy that has caused the most heated polemics and discussions everywhere. Certainly this interest is understandable, since China is today 80 percent agricultural.

Interview with a Minister of Agriculture

Before reporting on my visits to several Chinese communes, I would like to record an interview I had with the Vice-Minister of Agriculture, Mr. Wei Chen-hu. He began our interview by summing up in broad outline the agrarian policy of the leaders of the New China, before and since the Liberation.

"The reform was under way," said Minister Wei, "even quite awhile before we controlled the whole of our national territory. It was applied in the regions where we had influence and kept pace with our military advance. We always tried to adapt it to the peasants' immediate needs, lightening their burdens and interesting them in the changes. An agrarian reform to be successful must involve the peasant and interest him. It must emerge from the innermost depths of the country itself, from the aspirations of the peasant masses. No academic approach, no empty demagogy."

As the Vice-Minister continued speaking, I took rapid notes. The following is a paraphrase of his remarks.

"During the period of the war with Japan, we applied a policy of reducing rents and taxes. The miserable condition of the peasant masses had to be alleviated. This was the most urgent task. We did the same thing when Chiang Kai-shek unleashed the Civil War. In each zone we occupied, we helped the peasantry. In that way the peasant masses were on our side when the moment of Liberation came. By 1949 a great deal of water had already gone under the bridge. The peasant knew who had defended and aided him. The support of the peasants enormously facilitated our task during the first difficult years that followed the taking of power. Our peasant policy had contributed decisively to the triumph of the Revolution; it contributed afterward to its consolidation.

"The test that in the last analysis decides the fate of a revolutionary party is its ability to solve the problem of land," said Mr. Wei with conviction. "The agrarian reform required a very clear conception of what should be done, and a high sense of responsibility in doing it. One does not play at agrarian reform with impunity.

"The first step on a national scale was to take rural property out of the hands of the class that, from time immemorial, had been exploiting the Chinese peasant. We confiscated, therefore, the landlords' properties and distributed the land among the peasants. The struggle was directed against the *ruling* class of landowners. As for the rich peasants, we confiscated only that part of their land which they rented out. The middle-income peasants, who formed 20 percent of the peasantry, had also been victimized by the large landowners and so they, too, aided the agrarian reform. We took those circumstances into account and protected their land. As a result of this policy we had the support of the poor and middle-income peasants who together constituted 90 percent of the country population, and we were able to isolate the land-owning class. Actually, in redistributing the land, we even gave the landowners a parcel the same size as that given to the poor peasants, so that they, too, could become farmers.

"We did not commit the error of thinking that we were doing the peasant masses a favor. We convinced them that the thorough realization of the agrarian reform was in their own interest as well as that of the nation and of the Revolution, and we impressed upon them that no reform could be accomplished by decree alone, but *could* be successfully accomplished through the efforts of the people.

"The agrarian reform mobilized the peasants and gave them a political consciousness. Thanks to this, they have lifted their heads and established their own power. A very close relationship has been established between the peasant masses and the regime which came to liberate them. Our revolutionary forces counted on the peasants' support. It was a basic factor.

"Our primary responsibility was to keep the needs of China in mind, to adapt to them, to search for a realistic solution to each new problem that arose. It would not have done the peasant much good to be given the land if he didn't know what to do with it. It was necessary to place in his hands not only the means for cultivating it profitably, but also the methods and principles that would help him to succeed now that he had to make out on his own without a master to 'guide' him. This is how the principle and practice of cooperation made headway in the Chinese countryside.

"The peasants enthusiastically set out down the road of cooperation. The mutual-aid groups prepared the way for the cooperatives, which were based on the knowledge already acquired by the peasant of the advantages of collective labor over individual labor.

"The first cooperatives were semi-socialist in character; the land continued to be private property. But the advanced cooperatives which followed were essentially socialist in organization and structure. The principle of remuneration for work done prevailed.

"Gradually we moved forward. By 1956 the cooperatives completely dominated the countryside—with the exception of Tibet and certain territories of the national minorities. The most palpable result was an increase in agricultural production. The goals assigned to agriculture in the First Five-Year Plan (1953-1957) were fulfilled in advance."

After giving me this background, Minister Wei approached the question of the People's Communes.

"The very development of the forces of production," he said, "introduced into the countryside a series of problems that had to be solved. Irrigation, for example. The hydraulic projects required an effort that in many cases even the advanced cooperatives were not able to face. The same thing was true of the means of transportation. More tractors were needed, and many cooperatives could not afford them. Chairman Mao and the Central Committee of the Communist Party examined the situation and approved the proposal, supported by numerous demands from the provinces, to create a broader organization with greater possibilities of modernizing and mechanizing agriculture than the advanced cooperatives possessed. But the initiative for this change actually came from the peasants themselves.

"The People's Communes have not been 'forced,' as is said outside of China. How could hundreds of millions of peasants be forced to form communes, when they are armed?" (One of the characteristics of the communes is that they have their own militia and weapons.)

At the conclusion of our talk, Minister Wei assured me that the communes were not a matter of material progress alone. By making the responsibilities of the peasant masses greater and more varied, the communes constitute an important school of political education. Farming is no longer just a matter of sowing and harvesting the grain, but of manufacturing at least part of the material necessary for local construction of dams, canals, bridges, highways, and all kinds of simple utensils for household use. In addition, the communes are responsible for organizing education for their members.

"The People's Communes," said the Vice Minister of Agriculture emphatically, "are the backbone of socialist unity in the countryside. Some through lack of comprehension and others through ill will have tried to minimize their importance by saying they were 'imposed' by the Chinese Communist Party. Others say they function poorly. Of course, some communes have lagged behind in comparison with others. But they are all trying to improve the quality of their work. And, in any case, the fact that some communes are poor does not condemn the institution itself. There is no doubt that the communes have accelerated socialist construction, not hampered it. They represent one more step in the great work of transforming the Chinese countryside and of achieving the aims of the Revolution by degrees."

Commune Administration

For administrative purposes, the Chinese commune has a tripartite structure. First, there is an *administrative committee,* which is responsible for making advance proposals for production. These proposals are passed on to *production brigades.* The plans are discussed by an assembly of brigade representatives and there the work is distributed among the *work teams.* The work teams, in turn, have a chance to make suggestions, after which the administrative committee and the brigades agree on a definitive plan.

The administrative committee has the right to control the

brigades' production, but it also has the responsibility of helping them to solve problems that arise in connection with production. It must make sure that the industrial enterprises belonging to the commune function for the benefit of agriculture and that the commune does not undertake any plan for its own aggrandizement that is not in line with actual possibilities.

On the other hand, the brigades' production plan is based on the plan of the work teams. The brigades, finally, must yield certain rights to the teams in production and management. Through this procedure, the final plan has taken into account the interests of the state, of the commune and of the individual.

Any drawbacks in the procedure derive not from excessive despotism, but rather from excessive discussion. In fact, Peking recommended recently that the various assemblies of communal membership be held at longer intervals and that special care be devoted to the preparation of the agenda to keep the debate from being prolonged unnecessarily, thus interfering with the farm work.

The land as a whole is the property of the commune, which in turn divides it among the brigades. Each brigade uses the land assigned to it as its own, with the limitation that it may not sell or rent any part of it. Nevertheless, the houses in which commune members live are their own personal property; they may sell or rent them as they please. In the same way, whatever they produce on the small piece of land around the house belongs to them without restriction.

Communal enterprises, such as projects for water conservation, irrigation, electrical energy, belong to the commune as a whole; but in many cases the brigade owns the tractors and trucks. As for the work implements, they are the property of the members of the work teams. In general, the principles regarding property ownership are becoming steadily more flexible, with the evident purpose of meeting the centuries-old desire of the peasant to own something himself.

To give the reader an idea of how the profits are divided among the families that compose the commune, let me describe a scene that we witnessed. A certain commune we visited was in the process of distributing the autumn grain allotments, and a discussion was taking place among the members of Team Number Seven of the Ninth Brigade. Most of the 65 families that made up this team had filled the daily quotas assigned to them, but others had not done so, and the team was examining the reasons that were given for the failures. Some workers, it turned out, had had to stay at home because of family illnesses; some women became pregnant after the quota was assigned.

In cases where the reasons were considered valid, the share of the profits was the same as for those who had filled their quotas. In three cases, however, the excuses given were rejected, the team attributing nonfulfillment to bad habits left over from the old society, to egotism, to a lack of collective feeling. Therefore, these families were not considered qualified to receive the full grain allotment.

But there also existed quite different cases—members who worked hard and overfilled their quotas. They were rewarded with an extra allotment of rice, extra clothing coupons or coupons for consumer goods.

In all communes, members have the right to any supplementary benefits they can earn from working on their own private plots of ground during their free time. After work hours many members cultivate their own gardens or raise a pig or some chickens. The income they make from such efforts is their own to do with as they please.

Complete collective ownership based on the commune has been left for a later stage, when mechanization and modernization of agriculture will permit a transition to the socialist principle "from each according to his ability, to each according to his needs."

The Chinese leaders insist that even after the transition from communal ownership to ownership by the entire people, the communes should, during an inevitable historical period, continue the system of distribution "to each according to his work," because the products of society will still not be sufficiently abundant to permit the realization of full communism. This is stated quite clearly in the resolution, "On Some Questions Pertaining to the People's Communes," adopted in the Sixth

Session of the Central Committee of the Chinese Communist Party.

Such terms as "work brigades" and "militarization," the latter term originating in the communes themselves, gave rise in other countries to the erroneous impression that commune members lived a barracks-like existence. But, as explained in the September, 1958 issue of *Hongqi,* a bimonthly of the Chinese Communist Party, "To be organized militarily obviously does not mean that peasants are to live in a kind of barracks, nor does it mean that they are to be given the rank of generals, colonels or lieutenants! It simply means that the rapid expansion of agriculture requires the peasants to strengthen their degree of organization, to act more rapidly and with greater discipline in order to be able to develop on a vaster scale all of their capacities for the benefit of themselves and their country."

That the communes have resulted in the "destruction of family life" is a theme particularly popular in the occidental press. Happily the facts belie the allegations; there are no "dormitories for men" and "dormitories for women," as has been frequently alleged abroad. The people in the communes laugh when they are told what has been said about them. The director of one of the communes in the Shanghai region said while showing me the communal hospital: "You see, here are only women waiting to be mothers. It is the one 'sickness' that exists here—and hardly a testimonial to the 'destruction of family life'!"

The creation of the communes was the response to a real need. It was not the result of a worsening in the peasant's condition, but rather of an improvement. Already living better under the regime of the cooperatives, he wanted to advance still further in material well-being. He also wanted to serve his country, to help make China the great nation that it is already becoming. A current of elevated national feeling is making its way to the remotest places in the interior, and the work brigade that strives to increase the quality and quantity of the products taken from the earth knows that it is working not only for its own benefit, but also for the future of China.

Near the end of 1961, while I was still in China, a discussion

was going on about the role of the production brigades as
independent working units in the people's communes. This was
surely what gave rise to erroneous reports abroad that the
Chinese leaders, having recognized the failure of the communes,
had decided to abandon them in favor of the advanced cooperatives, which had preceded them. The cooperatives and
the brigades, and in the last analysis, the communes themselves,
were, according to this interpretation, one and the same thing
with different labels. In a word, the communes "had lived,"
as some French commentators said in performing an autopsy
on them.

But these commentators were forgetting the existence of
the principle which had presided over the creation of the
communes, according to which "the superstructure changes
while the basic framework remains unaltered."

To understand the nature of the People's Communes, it
is necessary to observe their development in stages—that is, in a
constructive process of advances, of halts in the road, of "rectifications in the style of work," (to employ an expression already
deeply rooted in the terminology of the Chinese leaders and
planners).

The communes are developing by steps, and there are two
main stages in that process: the socialist stage and the communist
stage. The socialist stage itself is divided into two phases—the
first wherein ownership is vested in the communal membership
and the second when all communes (and all means of production) will be owned by all the people of the country. The first
communal-ownership stage embraces two others: property rights
vested in the brigades, and property rights vested in the commune
as a whole.

It is because this evolutionary process has been lost sight
of that so many inexact things have been written about the
People's Communes.

The principle of the gradual transformation of agriculture
was defended by Mao Tse-tung even before the establishment of
the present regime. In 1943 Mao declared that "the way for
the peasants to end their poverty is to collectivize progressively."
This became a fundamental idea in the triumphant Revolution.

Article 34 of the Common Program (the provisional constitution of China) foresaw the gradual transformation of agriculture, beginning with the most elementary manifestations of mutual aid and proceeding to the advanced cooperatives.

Throughout its history of more than 30 centuries, China has passed through national crises on a scale that would have sunk any other people into an abyss beyond hope of escape. In the most difficult periods it found its vigor welling up from an inexhaustible source of energy: the peasantry

It is the peasantry which is proving today, through the communes, that a crisis such as that brought on by the natural disasters of 1959, 1960 and 1961 will always find in the people who are still close to the land a fiber and tenacity tough enough to overcome all difficulties.

Visit to "October Commune"

October Commune is an hour's automobile ride from Nanking. Its director, Li Chun-wen, briefed us on its origin and its present condition before we began a visit that lasted all day, interrupted only for lunch in the communal dining hall and a short nap. (In many places in China a nap has been incorporated into the work day, and has proven very effective in renewing a worker's energy.)

The commune, founded in September of 1958, was based on seven advanced cooperatives. "For a long time," the director told us, "we had felt the need for a more complete rural organization than the cooperative. The advanced cooperative was a great improvement over the old type, but it was not enough to supply the growing demands for agricultural production. For example, one cooperative, now a part of this commune, found itself without enough funds to buy a tractor. Another, also incorporated today in this commune, lacked a work force large enough to carry out an irrigation project. The peasants began to talk the matter over among themselves and to tell each other that it was necessary to get together in order to do things on a larger scale.

"Action began in the summer of 1958 when one of the advanced cooperatives recognized that it could not fight alone against the drought. Its members discussed the problem with members of other cooperatives in the same area. Then seven advanced cooperatives sent petitions with 10,000 signatures in all to the People's Committee of the district. The People's Committee examined the petition and then, in view of the magnitude of the movement, convoked an assembly attended by all the members of the seven cooperatives. The October Commune was thus born and the decision was celebrated in typical Chinese style, amid shooting skyrockets and the clamor of cymbals and drums.

"In all, the October Commune today contains 6,400 families and 32,000 members, that is, a small production army from which only children are excluded. Naturally, however, the children begin very early to grow familiar with farm work; they are the farmers of tomorrow. A section of the clinic is devoted to them, but it is not very busy. There are few illnesses among the children of the commune."

With the administrative personnel we reviewed some data which indicated how agriculture had developed in this region. Before the Liberation, the average income of a poor peasant in the area was the equivalent of 30 of today's yuan (about $13) a year; the more wealthy peasants made up to twice as much. "In one village of this commune," said the director, "composed of 23 peasant families, all of them would work for an entire year only to wind up by having to give the harvest to the landlord who was master and money lender at the same time."

"And what did they eat?" we asked.

"Roots, cereal husks, and poor quality vegetables. Real eating was only for the landlords and the rich peasants."

The total cereal production in this zone between 1949, on the eve of the proclamation of the People's Republic, and 1958, the year the October Commune was created, had increased 82 percent per *mu*. (A *mu* is equal to one-sixth of an acre.) The peasants' average income had reached 80 yuan, that is, it had passed the level achieved by fairly wealthy peasants before the Liberation. At the time of my visit (in 1961) the members of the commune received, on the average, about 100 yuan a year from the distribution of collective earnings. In addition, each member owns a small parcel of land and any earnings he makes from this plot of ground are his own.

As we toured the area of the commune in the director's car, he described what had been accomplished since its formation. The members had built 20 medium and small reservoirs, working on them during the periods of least activity in the fields. The reservoirs, designed mainly to limit the destructive effects of severe drought are also a source of fish. The fish make the members' meals more varied and nourishing, and are also sold in the market. In 1960 the reservoirs produced 700,000 fish; in 1961, a million.

"More than 30 percent of the cultivated land can now be irrigated with the water from these reservoirs," the director told me. "The waters of the Yangtze can also be directed onto the land through three small rivers and the canals which have been built.

"In the last two years we have bought a considerable amount of agricultural machinery that, before the founding of the commune, we would not have been able to finance. We also have our own repair shop."

We visited the shop. Its chief function was to repair farm tools. Beside it we saw a small cement factory that draws upon the nearby mountains for the required stone and gravel. In a small ceramics factory we saw the finishing touches being given to chocolate cups, plates, small pitchers, everything that a peasant home needs—all of it very simple, but attractive in form and color. There was also a carpentry shop, and even a fan factory. The heat that scorched us as we went from one end of the commune to the other was proof enough of the need for fans. The sun beat down like a hammer.

We do not wish to exaggerate: these were small shops and tiny factories. But they were of great value, both material and psychological, to the peasants. The communal industry has little by little created a kind of rural autonomy, providing the most indispensable items in general use and lessening the burden of large industry. "But we are very careful," observed the director, "to put what is first, first; and the first thing here is work on the land."

The members of this commune hold an assembly every six months, the production brigades every three months, and the work teams every month. "We are a new institution," Li Chun-wen told us, "and we are likely to commit errors. We are aware of the difficulties that await us, realizing that our production is still carried on, in part, by old methods. But we are slowly beginning to mechanize. We learn and we correct our mistakes."

In the dining room where we ate our mid-day meal, we were surrounded by tables occupied by the farmers, some by whole families. The members of the commune are free to eat either in the communal dining room or in their own houses. It is not true, as has been said abroad, that the communal dining room is imposed on the peasants and is one more sign of their "barracks-type life." Generally, they eat one meal a day in the communal dining room and the other two at home. It depends on the time of year and on the work in progress. "In the most active period of harvesting," the head of the dining room told us, "the families turn their foodstuffs over to the collective dining room and eat here because it is more convenient."

We saw houses under construction. It had been decided that straw houses were to disappear entirely. We visited the schools. Along with the children, some old people were learning to read and write or acquiring some rudimentary notions of history and geography, or learning to add and subtract. More than 80 percent of the members of the commune are now literate.

Besides the primary schools the commune boasted an advanced secondary school with a library and a very good laboratory, a movie projector and a radio room. It also had a clinic with about 50 beds. Each work team had its nurse. In one of the rooms of the clinic we saw a couple of farmers being treated with acupuncture. But in the small pharmacy, together with traditional herb preparations, were the most modern antibiotics.

Of course, we did not carry out an American-type opinion poll to find out whether the peasants approved of the commune or not, but they seemed satisfied. One of their songs says, "Happiness flows and flows here like the waters of the rivers."

The director of the October Commune gave the impression

of being a man who knew what he was doing. To direct a commune well is no mean feat; it can be more difficult than running a factory. A commune, as we have seen, comprises not only the land, but also small factories manufacturing steel, cement and parts for farm machinery. The director must also organize trade and take care of the thousand details of everyday life in common. It is not enough for him to know his own trade as a farmer; he also must be a good organizer and administrator.

Within the General Line that gives the communes, as their basic assignment, the responsibility for fulfilling the new needs of Chinese agriculture, a commune director has broad freedom of initiative. Some directors, on finding that capital had tripled in the first year of the commune's existence, invested the increase in expanding the means of production. This was done with the unanimous approval of the members and without getting bogged down in the details of ownership of the products. The benefits went to the commune itself; the central government collected no extra taxes. On the other hand, some directors lacked the necessary initiative to develop the commune substantially and were satisfied with slow but safe progress.

It must be said that there have been, unquestionably, serious retrogressions in production in some of the communes, due largely to the prolonged period of adverse weather conditions. There have also been expressions of peasant discontent with the malfunction of certain communes, and in some cases with the institution itself. But the reports of "violent manifestations" featured in the hostile press outside China were false.

The Huangtukang Commune

Since the level of advance in some communes is much greater than in others, one must visit several of them in order to form an accurate picture of the institution as a whole.

The Huangtukang Commune is located half an hour from Peking. Founded on August 28, 1958, it is composed of 6,000 families and a total of 26,000 persons. Devoted principally to the production of vegetables and flowers, together with some grain, it covers an area quite large for a commune of this kind—six miles long by five miles wide. Here a development has occurred that has established a precedent for the most prosperous communes. The concentration of labor and the output of the collective effort permitted the commune to tackle successfully the problem of mechanization. With its own funds, it has bought 560 electric pumps, 11 tractors, and eight trucks, in addition to 500 carts that travel from the commune to Peking.

In the seven months prior to our visit, that is, from January to August, 1961, the commune's income had increased by 18 percent compared with the preceding year. And this in spite of the torrential rains in the Peking region which had caused considerable damage to the vegetables.

As we walked across a field of flowers we heard about the future of the communes and the "need to learn from experience," a phrase very characteristic of Chinese farmers. The comments of the director, Ying Wei-chen, anticipated readjustments which were actually made a year later and which caused the rumor outside of China that the communes were being dismantled. He told us what had been done to eliminate or reduce the damaging effects of heavy rains and severe droughts. "In the years to come," he said, "we shall not have to fear either drought or floods."

"In the year 1946," added Director Ying, "there was a great drought in this very zone. The people were left without grain. The only clothes we had were those on our backs. What poverty! Of some 70 families who were working the land, more than two thirds fled or became beggars to keep from starving to death! There were also families who had to sell their children. Those who managed to subsist ate whatever they could find. Rice husks were a luxury. And all because the peasants did not own land and the landlord owned the peasants.

"This is not just empty talk," he continued. "I myself lived through it all. Since 1939 I had worked for the local political boss, who resented it when a person so much as opened his mouth to eat, though heaven knows what we had to put in our mouths was little enough! That was the way most of us lived. And that is why, when the agrarian reform began after the Liberation, all of us were behind the government. There was no need to force us either to join a mutual-aid team or, later, a cooperative. Everyone understood that it was the beginning of the end of poverty."

Next he explained the process followed by the peasant association. "We began by forming a mutual-aid team. At the start there were only three families in the group. The government lent us the most necessary items. By 1952 there were already eight families. The peasants' resistance to joining with others to work and share the profits was still great. But they saw that we were making progress. From 200 yuan, which were the average earnings in 1951, we moved to 308 yuan in 1952. There was not only enough to buy food, but also clothes and shoes, something we had never had before. That convinced the skeptics.

"By 1953 our team had become a cooperative, including 33 families, and our average annual income had increased to 410 yuan. In 1955 the cooperative was composed of 296 families. The average income of the farmers continued to increase. In 1956 some of the cooperatives joined together and formed an advanced cooperative. Now the landlords themselves, the old rich peasants, wanted to enter it. A distinction was made: those who had treated the peasants decently were admitted as full members and those who had not treated them well became 'half members'—that is, members with restricted rights in the administration of the cooperative. Through the efforts of the advanced cooperative, production continued to increase during the 1956-1958 period until the commune was formed."

"And what difference did you notice when the commune was created?" I asked.

"A very great difference," he replied. "In the first place, work became easier for the peasant. It isn't that we have stopped working hard, but mechanization has put an end to much unnecessary effort. Seeding was previously done by hand; today it is done with the tractor. Previously the peasants carried in baskets, and on foot, what they had to take to the market. Now trucks take care of it. The machines have ended a great amount of physical labor."

After crossing the five great flower gardens we admired the modern housing put up for the members of the commune. The housing summed up all that the director had been telling us from his own experience about the transformation which has taken place in the lives of the Chinese peasants. "If they had told me in 1939," he said, "that I was going to be able to live this way, I would have thought they were making fun of me."

The members of the commune have organized their social services very competently here. A clinical brigade with 15 doctors and nurses takes care of some 1,700 families. Half of the houses, now mostly of brick and built since the founding of the commune, have radio sets. Education has also moved ahead; 28 primary schools with a total of 10,000 students and two secondary schools with 1,400 students are part of the commune. For more advanced courses, students are sent to Peking.

The female members of the commune have the right to rest six days a month, two days more than the men, so that they can take care of family matters. Besides that, pregnant women enjoy the maternity care available in all of China.

The Ma Chiao Commune

The Ma Chiao Commune, located an hour's drive outside of Shanghai, is made up of 10,650 families with 48,000 members. Its main product is rice. Here mechanization was well advanced: there were 28 tractors, one of 50 horsepower that could plow more than 150 *mus* (25 acres) of land a day. "With the ox that was used by one of the small cooperatives, now part of our commune," one of our companions informed us, "it was possible to plow only five *mus* a day."

We crossed a great rice field. The crop was flourishing, because the electrical irrigation system which this commune uses had recently been expanded. Now there were two crops a year, one of rice and the other of wheat.

"Without the commune," the advising agronomist told us, "there would be no electrical irrigation. Even an advanced cooperative would have been unable to accumulate the necessary funds to electrify irrigation." And he added: "Before, if the drought were prolonged and severe, 18,000 laborers would have been needed to deal with the situation. Now a few hundred are enough."

Need for Mechanization

Naturally, the need of the Chinese countryside for mechanization is very great. Agriculture has been waiting with age-old patience until it could be supplied with the tools and machinery required if the task of feeding a nation of such dimensions is to be performed adequately. Though in the last 15 years the electrical energy used on farms has increased 65 times, there is still a crying need for more electric power. Tractors are also needed desperately. In both these areas each year represents a new advance, but, of course, it will be some time before China's industry will be able to keep up with the need for machinery in the agricultural sector.

Still, little by little the communes are increasing their mechanized teams through the acquisition of new tractors purchased with their own funds, or in some cases with the aid of state loans. At the beginning of the Third Five-Year Plan (1963) there were 500 tractor stations in Heilungkiang province, which made it possible to mechanize the work of over a fifth of the area of the province. This meant 16,000 tractors and their corresponding repair shops among the communes themselves. Almost 40,000 peasants and demobilized soldiers had already been trained as tractor operators in 1961. These figures are impressive in a country in which technology was almost completely neglected in the past, even though agriculture was well served by the inexhaustible patience and industry of the Chinese peasant. But with such vast expanses of land to be cultivated, it will still require more time to meet the total demand for tractors. This is one of the many possibilities that would be opened up to American manufacturers if their government's policy toward China did not prevent the normal development of trade.

To fill the present gap in the availability of tractors and farm machines, the planners have adopted the intelligent measure of giving the peasant a margin of choice in the tools he uses. Many communes make their own tools for farm work. The small tools, the sickle, the pick, the hoe, and the harrow are intimately connected with the history of the Chinese countryside and will keep their usefulness even when agriculture is thoroughly mechanized.

Pest Control, Reclamation and Crop Rotation

One of the battles that the communes are waging in Kansu province, among others, is against the locust. Many rural plagues have been effectively combatted in the last few years. But the locust is an old and obstinate visitor. The *Chronicle of the Yuan Dynasty* records that in 1359, "during the fifth month, clouds of locusts covered the sun in the provinces of Shantung, Honan, Hotung, and Kwangtung, impeded the movement of men and horses, and filled the wells and canals, where they fell. In the eighth month the locust clouds swept across Hopei and crossed Pienliang, devouring all of the crops in their path."

More than 600 years have passed since then, but the Chinese peasants in some regions must still contend with this enemy. But the locust's capacity for destruction has almost ended. Today the peasants, armed with new exterminating methods devised by Chinese agronomists, have fought victoriously against some of the worst invasions on record. The extent of the area affected has diminished considerably and the density of the insect clouds has decreased from year to year. The places which provide the most favorable conditions for their reproduction have been located by entomologists, and thousands of acres of land near lakes, particularly propitious breeding grounds, have been transformed into fertile rice and wheat fields.

The progress made in agriculture since the Liberation can also be measured by the reclamation of areas which in the past were the most arid. As a single example, one may take the accomplishment in Shansi province, where bare mountain slopes have been turned into farm lands producing profitable crops. Unified planning and the rational utilization of land and labor power have narrowed the difference that existed between the parcel of land that was obviously fertile and one that was considered hopelessly sterile.

The effort expended is at times enormous. There are the

long vigils when the peasants work by lantern light to turn stony fields lying in unproductive abandonment into arable land, in order to seed it the following day. But the effort pays, and the stories one hears of what these farmers have achieved, without allowing themselves to be dismayed by obstacles, reveal the confidence they evidently feel in the rewards that will follow.

In the communes special importance is given to the selection of seeds. The most varied types, imported from abroad and tested under the direction of the Ministry of Agriculture and the local scientific institutions, have been added to the seeds traditionally used in China. The result in many regions has been an improvement in the quality as well as the quantity of wheat, corn, rice and cotton harvests. Members of the communes are deeply interested in the selection which is made on their own experimental farms. One corner of the Ma Chiao commune, converted into a "botanical garden," where the oldest peasants can contribute their personal experience to the work of the scientists and qualified agronomists, is very popular among the members.

In the rotation of crops China finds itself reverting to a solidly rooted principle, as is indicated by a proverb repeated from time immemorial: "Changing crops is like applying fertilizer." But the application of that principle under qualified technical direction is taking place only today. One of the methods of rotation is to alternate crops of cereals that consume nitrogen with vegetables such as string beans that, on the contrary, add nitrogen to the soil; alternating wheat with cotton produces a different but similarly beneficial effect on the soil.

The Chinese Academy of Agricultural Sciences, with its affiliates in the provinces, is working hard to assure better crop selection in accordance with local conditions. It has been discovered, for example, in Shansi province that cotton grown in soil in which alfalfa was previously planted gives a greater yield.

The situation varies from one section to another. In the Northeast the combination of very extensive land and proportionally sparse population makes one crop a year the general rule. On the other hand, in the North the normal thing is three crops every two years, while in the South three crops a year can be counted upon. But agronomists are confident that the socialist planning of agriculture will in the end place the most backward regions on a par with the most advanced.

Health and Education

Another contribution toward raising the standard of living of the country population has been in the realm of health and education. Since the number of families gathered in the commune is much higher than in the advanced cooperative, the means for constructing schools are correspondingly greater.

Schools for the peasants' children are multiplying everywhere. Taking this development as a whole, it can be said that of every ten peasant children in China, eight are today being educated in the communes' primary schools. The course of study varies from four to six years, according to the province. A very interesting recent innovation was the establishment of boarding schools in isolated mountain regions where daily school attendance would otherwise be practically impossible for the children of families inhabiting remote villages.

Another educational development in the communes closely parallels a trend we had already noticed in the factories: the growing desire of workers to qualify for higher positions. The factory worker studies so that he can some day become an engineer. The ambitious peasant aims to become a qualified agronomist. As a result, the courses given by agricultural specialists are all well attended.

The Health Campaign has found a powerful aid in the communes. With their cooperation a great educational effort has been carried out. In the not too distant past, four million Chinese peasants died annually of infections caused by the use of human fertilizer. Although it maintained soil fertility in the face of thousands of years of intensive cultivation, the practice served as a constant threat to health and life itself. The Health Campaign has largely remedied the situation.

Until the Liberation superstitions were very widespread among the country people. Yunnan province, for example, is known for its splendid fruit trees and for its Tai girls, whose talent for dancing we had admired in a festival at the Palace of the Nationalities in Peking. But there demonology was commonly accepted. The peasant believed malaria to be an evil spread by women who had been transformed into demons. With each outbreak of an epidemic the houses and clothes of the "demon women" were burned, their land confiscated and the women and their families run out of the village. At times it was the landlord himself who, to punish the disobedience of some family, caused the rumor to spread that one of its members was possessed by the devil. For years those unfortunate women would wander from place to place, sometimes bearing children who inevitably died of malaria. Now both malaria and the superstition have been defeated.

The Communes and the Non-Agricultural Sector

As the time for reaping approaches, the yield that the harvest will provide is followed with an interest that is not limited just to the farmers. For many days it occupies much space in the press and on the radio.

It is difficult to imagine from outside of China the joy with which the news of a good harvest is received by the whole nation. In August of 1962 the first reports of the abundant rainfall, which in the North and Northeast of China eliminated the immediate danger that threatened the spring wheat, were met everywhere with extraordinary rejoicing. The same response came from the valley of the Yangtze. Finally, after three bitterly hard years, the agricultural prospects were improving. The rice crop looked good and the threat of a repetition of the tragic crop losses of the years 1959, 1960, and 1961 began to recede.

The results could be measured in an improved food situation. The communes contributed to the improvement by increasing their supply of vegetables to the cities. In some cities, as a result of the unexpected quantities of vegetables that reached the market, prices actually went down.

The communes have aroused widespread popular interest throughout the country. Efforts are made to help them in every way possible. The aid given by the army in the recent hard years of natural disasters is something that those who till the land will not forget. It linked soldiers and farmers in a way which rarely occurs in other countries. During the last year of the disaster period the army contributed more than 22.5 million work days to economic construction, and 80 percent of that effort was for agriculture: seeding, harvesting, building dikes and wells in the people's communes, etc.

In the communes we found officials and professional people of all kinds working with the peasants on the land. Everyone who is physically able must work in a commune or a factory for a brief period once a year. This idea of combining professional duties with manual labor is not an extravagant fancy of the present Chinese leaders. It is to be found in Marx, formulated with careful precision. Speaking of the ideal education of the future, Marx wrote (in Volume I of *Capital*): "In this education for all children of a certain age, productive labor will be united with intellectual instruction and physical education, not only as one of the means of increasing social production, but as the only way to form completely developed men."

The present Chinese method applies mainly to adults. An official of the Ministry of Foreign Affairs or a university professor helping to gather the harvest is already an important element of the agricultural scene. And according to what professional men and intellectuals who have participated in farm work say, they have not only felt pleasure in doing it, but in most cases have improved their health.

In the *Selected Works of Mao Tse-tung* one can read the following paragraph (in Vol. III). "There are two kinds of insufficient knowledge: that which is taken from books and that which is principally sensory and partial. Both are unilateral. Only the union of both can provide relatively complete knowledge." Lenin said the same thing in other words: "It is impossible to imagine the ideal of the future society without combining education with the productive labor of the young generation."

In the past few years discussions about education in China have revolved around this point, among others: "What is development in all its aspects?" The view that has prevailed is that complete development presupposes that students possess relatively wide knowledge, that they become skilled in various kinds of work, that they can "pass, in turn, from one branch

of production to another, according to the needs of society or
their own inclination." Adapting themselves to this orientation,
the Chinese "tend to make workers who are at the same time
farmers and farmers who are workers; to make civilians who do
military service, and demobilized soldiers who are producers;
to make cadres that take part in the work, and producers who
participate in management." This was the opinion Lu Ting-yi,
of the Central Committee of the Communist Party of China,
expressed at a recent conference on education.

This is only a tendency, an idea that, like all reforms in
China, is being applied gradually. But in it resides the explanation of the fact that we have found men working in the rice
fields who, while occupying a high position in their professions,
are peasants for a few weeks every year.

The Chinese leaders set the example. In one of the irrigation projects begun near the place where the Ming tombs are
located, Chairman Mao and the principal members of the
government recently fulfilled their obligation, working with the
energy regular workers normally display. Generals of the Liberation Army work in the communes, shoulder to shoulder with the
soldiers. They worked there most at the times when floods
threatened to ruin the crops. In fact the crops in some places
were saved, thanks to the aid given by the armed forces.

One of the reasons why the communes have been able, in
general, to survive the natural disasters and save crops that
would otherwise have been lost, is the principle of "simultaneity"
or "walking on two legs" which they have applied in their work.
The measures taken in the gravest periods to combat the drought
and preserve water and soil did not keep the communes from
going ahead with reforestation, cattle raising, and the subsidiary
production of farm tools and articles for use in the home, which
resulted at the end of the year in an increase in the communes'
income. In some places we were given figures on the money saved
by means of combined production—agrarian and industrial—and
it was considerable.

The commune permits a better distribution of labor power.
Communes and unemployment are mutually exclusive. Where a
commune is operating well there are no idle hands in the

surrounding area. In fact, one of the things that most impresses visitors from underdeveloped areas is to find that in China, a country of such a vast population, there is work for everyone and there is no unemployment.

Some day, when the history of "underdevelopment" is written, concerning the solution of which we have heard so many useless speeches in the United Nations in the last few years, the People's Republic of China will receive the credit it deserves for providing an example worthy to be taken into account in more ways than one.

Postscript

My appraisal of the People's Communes is confirmed by Raymond Scheyven, former Belgian minister and prominent Catholic leader, whom nobody can suspect of leftist leanings. Writing his impressions in the Paris daily, *Le Monde,* of a recent visit he made to China, M. Scheyven remarked: "The permanent mobilization made possible by the communes enabled China to wage a struggle of unprecedented efficiency against natural calamities. It is the first time that the Chinese peasants have been able to gather the necessary forces for what is called in Marxist language the 'taming of nature.' "

Elsewhere in his articles, M. Scheyven was sharply critical of certain other aspects of Peking's economic policy, but he was emphatic in asserting that general conditions in China are improving and he noted particularly the improvement in the standard of living of the Chinese masses.

A few days after the former Belgian minister left China, Vice-Mayor Chen Hung-yi of Peking made available some figures on commune productivity. Greater Peking includes an area of 6,485 square miles, of which a million acres are cultivated. Among the area's 7.4 million inhabitants, 300,000 are farmers. In communes and state farms, these 300,000 produce all the vegetables, fruits, eggs, milk, and most of the meat, as well as part of the grain, necessary to feed a population 24 times their number. Vegetables marketed in Peking rose from 300,000 metric tons in 1961 to 500,000 in 1962, and in 1963 were running 50 percent above 1962. It is no secret, of course, that

China's diet has always been poor in meat. Today the sale of meat and poultry is two and a half times greater than in 1962, while eggs are four times as plentiful. Milk, relatively new in China's diet, was 44 percent more abundant in 1963 than in the preceding year.

As mentioned earlier, some communes are much better administered than others. That raises the question whether, in writing this book, I am unduly accenting the positive. I do not pretend that all goes smoothly in today's China; all important Chinese leaders themselves admit that such an estimate would be wide of the mark. But I feel that since the world is flooded with all sorts of anti-Peking information (and on this point Americans are more generously served than any other people in the West), perhaps some emphasis on China's constructive achievements is in order. Moreover, some of the country's failures, which the Chinese leadership is the first to acknowledge, are subjected to a constant effort at correction. "Correction" is the favorite word of Mao Tse-tung and it plays an important role in the policies of the People's Republic of China.

7

THE GENERAL LINE

In China, 1962 was a year filled with interesting debates about past experiences and important decisions concerning what is called, in the construction of socialism, the General Line.

At the third session of the Second National People's Congress, held in Peking from March 27 to April 16 of that year, the report presented by Prime Minister Chou En-lai was discussed by the deputies for eleven days. In the plenary sessions, 164 representatives took the floor. That gives some idea of the broad proportions of a discussion which took place at a decisive time for the subsequent course of the People's Republic.

Both the People's Congress and the Consultative Assembly —the two main organs of the supreme government—convened at the same time. The Assembly is made up of representatives of non-government groups and organizations, including religious bodies, the various parties, the national capitalists—who, at the time, were still collecting interest on their investments—and the Chinese from abroad. The two organs deliberated separately, in different buildings, with the Assembly acting in an advisory capacity.

This time the session of the Consultative Assembly was attended by 897 members, plus 816 guests; all present had distinguished themselves by their work in different branches of national activity. Among the guests were former generals of Chiang Kai-shek who had been arrested and rehabilitated, and the last Emperor of China, Pu Yi. When one considers that, in all, three thousand persons were in attendance at these secret sessions, and that the sessions continued over a period of many days, it was extraordinary that there was not a single withdrawal of a delegate, advisor or guest, and not a single indiscretion.

It was only to be expected that such an event should inspire in the foreign press a wide variety of conjectures as to what had happened. And along with this artificially created confusion were stories attributing the secrecy of the deliberations to "the desire of the Peking government to hide the phenomenal failure of their whole economic policy, dramatized by the fugitives fleeing from hunger toward Hong Kong"—to quote one of the foreign press "experts."

I felt, on the contrary, that I was treading firm ground when I wrote about these events as they happened, in my newspaper reports. The material I had accumulated during my second visit to China, part of which forms the substance of this chapter, had given me a solid basis of fact from which to operate.

On many occasions, while writing this book, I have copied directly from jottings made in my notebooks "on the spot." What follows now are notes of this sort, based on several long conversations with Mr. Yung Lung-kuei, Vice Chairman of the China Council for the Promotion of International Trade, on the all-important problem of planning. I have broken into his story only briefly here and there with comments of my own which I have enclosed in parentheses.

"We will take as our point of departure," said Mr. Yung, "the situation in 1957, when you came to China for the first time. The two main phases of our Revolution had already been carried forward. The first was the democratic Revolution. Nothing solid could be undertaken without liquidating the remains of feudalism. After overcoming the reactionary regime of the Kuomintang, we founded the People's China, whose most immediate task was to clear away the last vestiges of feudalism, the privileges of the old society.

"This permitted us to cause sovereignty to pass into the hands of the Chinese people. A couple of statistics will illustrate what I mean. In old China there were 1,800 foreign-owned enterprises, including factories, mines, retail stores, ships. Today, with very few exceptions, these enterprises have passed into the hands of the people. And even the few that still remain in private hands must adapt themselves to the government's laws and policies.

"The People's China then put into motion the agrarian reform through which the feudal system of land ownership was completely destroyed. In so doing, however, we found it advisable politically, and also just, to establish a difference in treatment between two sectors of the old society: the proprietary class which had directly served the interests of foreign imperialism, and that other sector which, in the last analysis, had identified itself with the people against the foreign exploiters. The former comprises the bureaucratic bourgeoisie, the latter the national bourgeoisie.

"The former, taking advantage of the policy of the Kuomintang and the corruption that accompanied its rule, had accumulated considerable wealth through exploitation of their workers. From these we confiscated, without compensation, all the rural property in their hands. However, old landowners who were not guilty of crimes against the people were permitted to associate themselves with their local agricultural collectives.

"We likewise confiscated, without compensation, the industrial property of the bureaucratic bourgeoisie. With these enterprises in our hands, we were able to survive the blockade and the embargo.

"Toward the national bourgeoisie, who constituted 50 percent of the total, we followed a different policy—one of collaboration, giving them every opportunity to join the great effort undertaken by the Chinese people.

"Without first carrying out the Democratic Revolution, it would have been very difficult, perhaps impossible, to proceed to the Socialist Revolution."

The Socialist Revolution

"From 1949 to 1952 we laid the foundations for the new economy, reorganizing and reconstructing agriculture, stabilizing prices and balancing the budget. We reformed the confiscated enterprises at the same time.

"The First Five-Year Plan attained its main objectives, the first of which which was to open the way for the socialist transformation of society.

"As a result of the agrarian reform, the peasants became simultaneously workers and small landowners. Our policy then was designed to make sure that this process would be accompanied by an increase in agricultural production. This explains the rapid expansion of the cooperatives, the equivalent of the collective farms in the USSR. By the time you came to China for your first visit, 98 percent of the peasant holdings had been grouped into cooperatives.

"The figure was so impressive that the occidental press charged that we had *forced* the peasants into the cooperatives, just as later the same press charged that we used force to create the People's Communes. As if it were possible to force 550 million peasants to do anything!

"Agricultural production increased by 25 percent at that time—in itself proof that the peasant participation was indeed voluntary and that there was no sabotage.

"Yet the immense majority of the peasants were convinced that the agrarian reform was not enough; that everything depended on the kind of organization that went with it; and that only socialism would assure their prosperity.

"The second objective of the First Five-Year Plan was the transformation of the working situation of about five million individual artisans. They were organized into cooperatives on a voluntary basis; all problems concerning them were resolved by 1956.

Problem of the Bourgeoisie

"The third objective was the socialist transformation of the national bourgeoisie, which in essence was capitalist. Yet, as I have said, here was something very different from the bureaucratic bourgeoisie. The national bourgeoisie in old China had desired national prosperity; it had opposed imperialism and, in a certain sense, had also been victimized by the Kuomintang's repressive policies. Many of these bourgeoisie had from the very beginning supported the idea of ending the reactionary regime; when they were not actively on the side of the people, they were at least neutral. Naturally, the Revolution had to take this into account.

"In any case, their knowledge and experience in certain industrial activities, as well as their factories, were needed by the people of China. We therefore adopted a policy aimed, on the one hand, to eliminate the exploitative element from the national bourgeoisie and, on the other, to incorporate it as a class into our national effort.

"We did not confiscate their property, as we had that of the bureaucratic bourgeoisie. We chose a 'peaceful' transformation involving a minimum of force and without punitive intent on our part. Their enterprises were converted into 'joint enterprises' on the following basis: The government agreed that each national capitalist would receive five percent annual interest on his investments, tax free, on condition that the enterprises would be managed by the state. The capitalist himself could work for the enterprise, receiving a salary commensurate with his experience and ability, but of course he had to subordinate himself to state management. Moreover, the capitalist remained a full citizen, with his political rights guaranteed: he could vote and run for office.

"Today, some national capitalists are deputies in the Congress; a smaller number occupy posts in the government. For instance, two of them are Vice-Presidents of the Permanent Committee of the National People's Congress. The Minister of Light Industry is a former capitalist from Tientsin. When you visited Shanghai in 1957, you met the Vice-Mayor; today he is the Vice-Minister of the textile industry." (The reference was to Yung Yi-jen, whose dinner guests we had been in Shanghai. We had found him and his wife an attractive couple as well as lively conversationalists. Mr. Yung had told us how his father, the multimillionaire Yung Teh-sheng—who was once the subject of front-page stories in the American press because he had been held for $200,000 ransom by Shanghai kidnappers —had decided, despite his advanced age, to stay in China after the triumph of the Revolution. On the other hand, one of his brothers chose Hong Kong and the other Siam, where he had a factory. But Yung Yi-jen, staying on in Shanghai, saw his factories become part of a joint-ownership enterprise, under which he was guaranteed an annual dividend on his capital, and proceeded to carve out a brilliant career for himself under the new regime.)

"In the not too distant future," continued Mr. Yung Lung-kuei, "the national bourgeoisie will have been fused with the Chinese people living under socialism. Their way of seeing things will gradually have changed, not to mention that of their children, many of whom have enlisted enthusiastically in the youth organizations.

"By the end of 1957, the socialist system was definitely installed. That year we denounced certain errors in the practical application of our policy."

The Great Leap Forward

"This was on the eve of the Great Leap Forward that began, as you know, in 1958. In order properly to appreciate what an event which had such repercussions was like at the beginning, it is necessary to review the economic situation as it appeared in 1953 and again in 1957.

"Speaking in general terms, the total social investment of that period was 55 billion yuan [about $24 billion], of which 49.3 billion was supplied by the state. More than half of the investments went to build factories and mines. In all, we got 10,000 enterprises under way, of which 900 may be classified as large. Many were installed with the aid of the Soviet Union and other socialist countries. With their aid, we also developed our own technical forces. It was essential to do so; otherwise, to operate all that had been built we would have needed thousands of foreign experts.

"The First Five-Year Plan proved the effectiveness of socialist planning in an economically and industrially backward country. In comparison with 1952, the over-all industrial production in 1957 already showed an increase of 128 percent.

"The basis was now established for the Great Leap Forward.

"The end of the First Five-Year Plan brought up the question of raising the people's standard of living. Much had been done, but living conditions were still very poor. Even today we have not reached the level attained by many Western countries. But the effort to do so is constant and, during the last few years, has been intensified. We have committed errors, but we have not persisted in them; we have learned, and as we learned we rectified.

"Our low living standards called for a great push in production. This was the desire of the broad masses of the people, who wanted to see China transformed into a prosperous country. Thus was the Great Leap Forward inspired, and the masses threw themselves into the task with resolution.

"The main achievement of the Great Leap Forward has been the expansion of everything achieved during the First Five-Year Plan. We enlarged the basis for modernizing our industry and increased the productive capacity of our existing enterprises. With the development of the steel and iron industry, other vital sectors of the economy, such as transport, were extended in turn.

"In 1958, the first year of the Great Leap Forward, steel production had reached eight million tons; by 1959, 13½ million. I recall that when you and I talked in 1957, I told you that by 1962 we hoped to reach 12 million tons. Well, in 1960 we already produced 18 million tons.

"We were then certain of being able to raise production in other essential industries to the goals we had set. From that point on, we have been able to build all kinds of machinery which we previously had to import. Thanks to the Great Leap Forward, we are in a position, for instance, to build mining and hydraulic-plant equipment, on which agricultural progress depends in great part. In not too many years, China will be self-sufficient in the machine industry. You realize what this will mean for China!

"To get where we are, we have had to mobilize all the productive forces of the country. But this did not involve 'forced labor,' as the foreign press has irresponsibly reported, but socialist mobilization. Our General Line calls for full speed ahead to develop the economy in order to assure the greatest possible well-being of the masses. This requires a great and constant effort—the concept of full activity.

"The relative priorities to be given heavy industry, light industry, and agriculture are among our chief preoccupations. If at one time we found it necessary to place the emphasis on heavy industry, it was for reasons intimated earlier—to create a firm foundation for economic expansion. But even at the culminating point in the great industrial push, we never overlooked the important role of agriculture in our over-all economy.

"During the Great Leap Forward we worked at high speed —at a rate faster than that of the Five-Year Plan. But it must never be forgotten that the present accelerated rate of production would not have been possible except for the socialist basis that we laid down prior to 1958.

"I have already given you the production figures for steel— a 70 percent increase in the first two years of the Great Leap Forward. This has meant not only greater speed and better materials, but also better technical personnel. You have probably heard it said—and you will hear it often in your visits to factories, educational centers, and ministries—that half of our success depends upon the cadres. It is not enough to produce engineers, geologists, agronomists, architects, chemists; they must be good at their jobs. As production develops, we will need technicians capable of taking initiative without having to wait for instructions from Peking on every little detail.

"Thus, decentralization is favored insofar as it does not obstruct planning and is substantially in accord with the General Line. But for this we need cadres capable of carrying out tasks which previously had to be outlined in minutest detail. We need cadres that can 'walk on both legs' without falling." (To "walk on both legs" is an expression quickly grasped even by the relatively few remaining Chinese illiterates. The phrase is typical of the graphic quality of Chinese revolutionary language. It means, among other things, to combine modern technology with the traditional methods of the artisan. The production of "people's steel"—steel forged in rudimentary commune shops installed by peasants under the direction of experts from nearby technical centers—is an example of "walking on both legs.")

"The Soviet Union and other countries helped us to train our personnel. Today a Chinese engineer can do five times what he could do before the Liberation. By 1952, the same engineer, though able to do many new things, could not yet design a project independently. By 1957, he could design smelting furnaces of 350-ton capacity. Today he can make smelting furnaces of 1,500-cubic-meter capacity.

"The fact is that we no longer need Soviet and other foreign technicians in such large numbers.

"What, in sum, has the Great Leap Forward accomplished? We have already seen that our steel production goals were exceeded. So, too, were the goals in other sectors of the economy —coal, electrical energy, the construction of industrial machinery, wood, paper, textiles. In the vital machine-tool industry, we are now able to produce by ourselves 80 percent of what we need.

"We must still import many precision instruments and very heavy equipment. And we must also admit frankly that in various other aspects of production, we have not yet achieved the technical level of the highly industrialized nations. Nevertheless, it is not idle boasting when we say: 'In industry, China today is truly a great nation.' "

The Agricultural Problem

(My conversations with Mr. Yung on agriculture began with an exchange of impressions about the communes I had seen. Mr. Yung then proceeded to review the effects on agriculture of the natural disasters that, unfortunately for China, had not yet come to a close at the time we talked.)

"The devastating effects of three consecutive years of floods and droughts—some of them among the worst China has known in a hundred years—were not limited to agriculture. The effects were felt in industrial production, beginning with the textile industry, and in the general financing of the economy.

"Let us say, for example, that tobacco is sold at 50 cents a package and 25 percent of the price goes to the state. If one fewer package is produced, the state's income is cut by that much—and that much less is available for the financing of state production in other fields.

"It must be kept in mind that industrial production can be controlled by man; agricultural production, a biological process, is controlled in large measure by nature. Therefore, the re-establishment of production in agriculture may require one year, two years, three years or more, depending not only on our own efforts but on the weather.

"You have asked what the state is doing on a country-wide

scale to control natural disasters. To begin with, we are building water reservoirs, some of them gigantic in size. Some are finished, and others—as you saw in Anhwei province—are still under construction. Aside from the progress made on the great rivers— the Yellow River, the Yangtze, the Pearl River—work is going ahead on subsidiary streams, partly on the initiative of the communes.

"As a result of these efforts, the area under irrigation has increased by 30 to 50 percent in the last four years. But one cannot solve great problems in the twinkling of an eye! Even though many of the completed reservoirs are of enormous capacity, the continued drought has kept them from accumulating as much water as we had expected. As with agriculture, so too with flood control and irrigation projects—nature must help out."

The Communes

"It is not true, as some foreign commentators have alleged, that we have practically 'decapitated' the communes. We have adapted them to new circumstances as experience dictated, and in accordance with the demands and suggestions of the communes themselves.

"Aside from improving the techniques of farming, it is vital to arouse the enthusiasm of the farmers. An agrarian policy like ours, so new, so revolutionary, and involving as it does the abandonment of so many ancient concepts and customs, cannot be carried out without the support of the great majority of the farming population. In the last analysis, force is completely useless in dealing with such enormous masses; they can be moved only by conviction.

"You have been able to observe the spirit of the communes. In them, the concept of democratic centralism is firmly rooted. Their internal operation permits readjustment, the redistribution of functions, all without altering the basic structure.

"In some communes, the prudent limits of 'home industrialization' were exceeded. But such mistakes offer not the slightest reason for abandoning the principle of the commune; all that is required is adjustment to local conditions. There are communal industries, for example, that can make use of local products—fuel from neighboring coal mines, perhaps, or clay for the manufacture of ceramics. Our peasant population is so enormous that even a partial utilization by it of local resources can contribute significantly to the country's total industrial output.

"We don't encourage the communes to become entirely self-supporting, because that is not possible. There are materials that cannot be produced economically by the communes—cotton, for example, in the production of which native methods have definitely been surpassed. But we do encourage the communes to engage in those industrial activities that can be of service collectively to the members.

"The people's communes are here to stay, and they will be further developed and consolidated. But this will be done in such a way so as not to deflect them from their fundamental task, which is agriculture."

8

FOREIGN POLICY

In 1957 Premier Chou En-lai, who was then also Minister of Foreign Affairs, gave me a long interview. Since much of what he said is still timely and reveals the continuity of Chinese foreign policy, I shall quote him here at some length.

I asked the Premier whether the cold war did not constitute a kind of "prewar state" capable of erupting into a hot war at any time. The Premier thought not.

"In the past few years," he said, "we in China have taken the view that the world situation tends to diminish the threat of war. This does not mean that tensions do not continue. New ones arise constantly. They have their origin in the behavior of the United States, which fears a lessening of tension because that would support the movement for peace and react unfavorably upon Washington's policy of monopoly and control. Any trend toward peace might lead to a rupture of the Western alliance, and dreading this, the United States seeks to maintain a certain amount of tension—even at the risk of general war.

"Nevertheless, when the tension reaches a point at which war seems about to explode, it is the United States that tends to draw back. To date, the Americans are not yet ready to unleash a new world conflict. Of course, there is no guarantee against the unexpected; unforeseen incidents of a local character could expand beyond the control of the forces gambling with the tactics of intimidation. There is also the possibility that a handful of American jingoists could set fire to the world by deliberately spreading some local conflict. This is why we will not cease to be vigilant.

"In a word, the general situation tends toward a lessening of tensions, but there has been a succession of tension-filled incidents provoked by the forces opposed to peace."

Upon what did Chou base this picture of the world situation? On the decisions taken by the United States itself at various critical moments: (1) not to spread the Korean War; (2) to accept, albeit reluctantly, the ending of the Indochina war by peace treaty; (The premier was speaking, of course, before the United States decided to intervene unilaterally in South Vietnam.) (3) to refuse to back Chiang Kai-shek's desire to defend the small islands in the Taiwan Straits; (4) to beat a retreat instead of actively supporting the Hungarian revolt once the Soviet Union intervened; (5) to oppose the military operations of its allies during the Suez crisis. In the latter case Chou said the U.S. feared a spreading war in the Middle East which might cost her her imperialistic positions; hence the U.S. took advantage of the blunders of her allies and sought to replace them as master of the whole region.

Our conversation veered to the subject of China and the United Nations. The Premier's tone suddenly acquired a marked firmness. "Our position is definite: we will never join the United Nations as long as the representatives of Chiang Kai-shek are admitted. That applies to the specialized agencies as well as to the U.N. itself. To lend ourselves to the 'two Chinas' thesis would not be serving the cause of peace. It would mean adding one more element of confusion to an international situation that is already confused enough.

"No, we will never permit ourselves to propose such a maneuver to the Chinese people. Meanwhile, we do what we can outside of the United Nations in support of peace and international cooperation. We are making every effort to preserve the peace, even though we are convinced that should war break out the imperialists would be the losers, and the reconstruction of China would continue. But we do not want war; we want to cooperate with all countries—all, I say, without exception."

Closed Door of the U.N.

Peking constantly maintains its right to occupy the U.N. seat that belongs to China, but it will not agree to enter through the back door. When in July of 1962 the UNESCO conference on the protection of works of art in war met in Paris, it had "authorized the People's Republic of China by implication" to send a delegate. A Chinese foreign-affairs spokesman answered through a statement published in Peking:

"As long as the legitimate seat of China in the United Nations and in its dependent organizations is usurped by Chiang Kai-shek's clique, it is evident that China will not consent to participate in any U.N. activities, nor to sit at the same table with the representatives of said clique."

Nevertheless, China seeks the widest possible cultural contacts with each of the nations belonging to UNESCO. As an example, the Institute of Foreign Affairs of the Chinese People, presided over by the scholar and internationalist, Professor Chang Hsi-jo, who is assisted by Chou Keng-sheng and Wu Hsiao-ta, performs an excellent service by inviting to China such outstanding personalities as Pierre Mendès-France and Edgar Faure, as well as professors and experts in international affairs of the most diverse political affiliations.

In its relations with capitalist countries that do not maintain a systematic policy of hostility toward it, Peking behaves with an elasticity that at times leaves Western diplomats perplexed. The fact that Australia is capitalist and a member of SEATO does not prevent China from maintaining friendly relations. The same thing can be said of Pakistan, another SEATO member.

It is incorrect to think that every time the U.N. discusses the question of China's membership, Peking waits on pins and needles for the outcome. Within the U.N. or outside of it, China is determined to continue its task of reconstruction.

The Playgrounds of Djakarta

The Peking government is sensitive to any maneuver which seems to be aimed at making it swallow the fiction of "two Chinas." On the occasion of the fourth series of Asiatic games in Djakarta, Indonesia, in the summer of 1962, the Chinese press condemned the American press for playing up the "sporting spirit" and the idea of "non-political sports" while simultaneously insisting that the "two China" concept should be extended to the sports arena.

This was not the first time the question had arisen. In 1952 the International Olympic Commission, reacting to vigorous protest from Peking and the pressure of world opinion, had found itself obliged to invite China to the Fifteenth Olympiad. In 1954, the same body recognized the legal status of China's athletic organization, the Pan-Chinese Athletic Federation.

American reaction was prompt, and under U.S. pressure the Commission finally recognized Chiang Kai-shek's Olympic representation. China immediately announced that it no longer recognized the Commission, and broke off relations with it.

American Hostility

China has been the object of greater hostility on the part of the United States than has any other country, including the Soviet Union. The United States permitted its citizens to visit the USSR, and permitted trade with it, even before diplomatic relations between the two countries were established. But in the case of China, Washington not only decreed a trade embargo, but kept even such an internationally known figure as Mrs. Eleanor Roosevelt from visiting the country.

In reply to the American charge, repeated by other Western nations, that the New China is dominated by militarism, one might cite what Felix Greene has written in his book, *The Wall Has Two Sides*:

How many military bases is America maintaining on foreign soil? Hundreds. And China? None. . . .

America today spends $6 million *every hour* on military armaments. America spends in just sixteen days what China spends on her military requirements in the whole year. . . .

America spends 56.4 percent of its national budget on current military expenses, excluding the billions she gives to arm her allies. The Chinese spend 8.3 percent. . . .

Ten times more money is spent in America on its current military expenditures than for the combined expenditures on social security, education, health, and welfare. China spends 50 percent *more* on these items than on military expenditures. . . .

Commenting on the theory, so widespread abroad, that the Chinese leaders scorn "peaceful coexistence" and favor force as the way to settle international disputes, a foreign friend who has lived in Peking for some time said to me: "Look at Hong Kong.

Coexistence with Hong Kong is more real and tension there is less than in Berlin. In the case of China, someone ought to take on the job of writing the anti-legend."

In fact, some observers have begun to re-establish the good habit of approaching important issues with a degree of objectivity. As an example, Professor C. P. Fitzgerald, whose book *Revolution in China* won from the London *Times* the comment that it is a "most important contribution toward understanding the character and conduct of the Chinese People's Republic," wrote in that work:

"It is difficult for the West to admit that the Chinese people could have voluntarily accepted communism. It is difficult to accept as real the support given freely to a regime that denies freedom to some while it gives limited freedom to others. And, nevertheless, there is no doubt at all that the new system has the support of the people, has satisfied the aspirations of the educated, and has won the allegiance of men of religious temperament."

Professor Fitzgerald pays tribute to the Chinese tradition of conciliation and refutes the notion that under the present government the Chinese people have no possibility of expressing themselves freely either in foreign or domestic policy.

U-2 Over China

When the Chinese brought down an American U-2 plane carrying Formosa markings in September, 1962, a French information agency noted:

It would not have been worth while to send a U-2 through the skies over an underdeveloped country. It is because the Soviet Union and People's China are countries in the process of development . . . that the risk of sending U-2s over them is taken. By downing one, the Chinese Communists have secured their skies against the best aircraft. Have these defensive weapons been supplied to them by the USSR, or have the Chinese themselves developed them? The scond hypothesis should not be discarded.

Why send a U-2 over People's China? The approaching nuclear capacity of the country is the big worry of the United States. . . . They urgently need to discover if the nuclear powerhouse which can produce the plutonium indispensable for making the first Peking

A-bomb has been finished. But the CIA, and consequently the Kennedy government, will never see the negatives taken from the cameras of the destroyed aircraft. Will they dare send a second 'Formosan' U-2 on the mission?

Was the plane really "Formosan"? On August 2, 1961, Wu Pao-shih, a pilot in Chiang's air force, landed on Chinese soil during an exploratory flight over Fukien province. The New China News Agency printed his statement that "the U-2 planes stationed in Formosa are under the direct orders of the American military command."

The U-2 incident shook Chinese public opinion. The people reacted with a mixture of pride and indignation. The prevailing sentiment in Peking was that President Kennedy had dangerously extended his military policy in Asia. Activities of the spy plane were linked to the heavy movement of Chiang's forces from Taiwan to the coastal islands, including the Pescadores. And all of this was related, the Chinese were convinced, to American military activity in Thailand and Vietnam and was regarded by Peking as a concrete threat to China.

Peking's View of Washington

Rumors that circulate from time to time about an eventual change in United States policy towards China are greeted in Peking with a smile—that familiar smile reserved by the Chinese for any remark that seems to take too seriously the good intentions of the leader of the "free world." They know that the United States not only persists in denying China its rightful place in the United Nations, but that it is using its influence to keep other nations from recognizing or engaging in normal commercial relations with the People's Republic.

Chinese diplomacy sees through each move that is initiated against it in the United States. It realized from the outset that SEATO was created for the sole purpose of mobilizing against China those Asiatic countries that allow themselves to be led by the nose by Washington.

United States policy has not only refused to recognize China, and opposed its membership in the U.N.; it has also resisted every

attempt by any third nation to associate Washington even in-
directly with negotiations involving Peking.

This is what happened in the case of the proposal made by
Prince Norodom Sihanouk, Chief of State of Cambodia, that
his country be granted a guarantee of neutrality similar to that
obtained by Laos following the 14-nation conference in Geneva.
A State Department spokesman immediately pointed out the
"obvious difficulty" entailed by a plan that meant gathering
around the same conference table not only the Soviet Union,
but "Communist China and North Vietnam, both nations not
recognized by the United States." And they apparently tried to
convince Prince Sihanouk that his best course was to reach
an understanding with Thailand and South Vietnam—that is,
to accept as allies precisely the two neighboring nations whose
aggressive conduct had led Cambodia to propose a protective
neutrality guarantee in the first place.

The United States not only applied a trade embargo to
China, but also tried to induce other Western countries to adopt
one. The American government sought unsuccessfully to dissuade
the British from selling aircraft to Peking. Similarly, Washington
looked on disapprovingly as, following China's purchases of grain
from Canada, steps were taken to open trade relations between
China and Australia. The Americans feared that England's
eventual entry into the Common Market would lead Australia
to increase its interest in the Chinese market.

British businessmen, cleverer than their American colleagues,
rejected from the outset the American fantasy that the Peking
regime was doomed to early collapse. On my second trip, I saw
more British trade representatives in the Shanghai Hotel than I
had on my first. These visitors were not impressed by the theory,
current in the United States, that "China can't buy because it
has nothing to pay with."

Trade with the West

So the British are discovering for themselves the possibilities
of trade relations which would benefit both countries. Recently
China purchased twenty British Viscounts for its airlines. China
already had planes of a similar type, the Russian-made Ilyushin

18, in which we made many trips to Nanking, Shanghai, and other places. But with the increase in domestic air traffic, Peking wanted more than one source for its aircraft, and the deal with Britain was consummated.

The two countries have also exchanged numerous commercial delegations and groups of experts, thus laying the foundation for a broader cooperation that is full of promise for the future. In the second half of 1961, visits by Chinese specialists to Great Britain began to be more frequent. A delegation led by the Vice-Director of China's Civil Aviation Administration studied the latest advances in British aeronautic laboratories and factories; a number of refrigeration experts studied English methods for measuring and controlling low temperatures. In 1962, a group of six petroleum engineers, led by Ling A-hua, General Secretary of the Chinese Association of Chemistry and Chemical Engineering, visited the British Exposition of Chemical and Petroleum Engineering. In interviews with various British experts, they familiarized themselves with new methods used in the exploitation of petroleum and related activities.

Still another group of Chinese specialists went to London in the summer of 1962. This time the object of study was British shipbuilding, and the Chinese experts were headed by Cheng Hsin, director of the Engineering Department of the China Ocean Shipping Company.

Maurice Tollit, director of a British export consortium comprised of some 80 companies, thinks that "the possibilities are enormous" in Anglo-Chinese trade. Tollit has pointed out that when the consortium's export plans were in preparation, not too much hope was held out for the China market. "But," he continued, "we decided to study the matter on the spot. We were pleasantly surprised. We met men of great efficiency, with a high concept of commercial morality and anxious to expand their commercial contacts abroad. Trade between the consortium [Guest, Keen and Nettlefolds] and China followed immediately, and with the steady confidence on our part that it can be considerably developed in the future. In a word, we found a first-class market for British industry."

To the annoyance of strategists who planned China's isola-

tion, newspapermen in Hong Kong have been obliged, from time
to time, to report on "the active commercial relations of Communist China with the Western world." This was the title of a
column which appeared in *La Vanguardia* of Barcelona, on Aug.
19, 1962, by its Hong Kong correspondent, José Chang. Describing how useful for China is the British enclave of Hong
Kong, Mr. Chang wrote:

The port of Hong Kong is engaged in a constant loading and
unloading of merchandise. Hundreds of ships a day unload the
most varied cargoes which are trans-shipped to all parts of the
world by China's national import and export center located in
Peking.

Under the impulse of this organism, whose tentacles reach
throughout the world, new bilateral agreements of indubitable
importance are being established with countries which, even though
they make anti-Communist political statements in the U.N., have
found in their powerful commercial firms the screen behind which
they operate.

Mr. Chang, who cannot be accused of Communist sym-
pathies, estimates that China's daily operations in Hong Kong
amount to $162 million.

The fact is that, despite the American embargo, Chinese
trade is increasing in all directions. The whole sterling area is
attracted by the possibilities. In 1961, the scarcity of grain resulting from bad crops caused China to buy $125 million worth
of wheat from Australia and $113 million from Canada; other
purchases of grain were made in Australia, Canada, and France;
and flour was purchased from Germany. And $50 million worth
of foodstuffs was purchased that year from the Soviet Union.

Relations with Japan

A delegation from Japan was staying at the Hotel Peking
while we were there. To several of its members I expressed my
regret at not having been able to accept the invitation of Tokyo's
most important peace group—represented in the delegation—to
attend an anti-bomb demonstration in Japan. The invitation had
chased after me from Moscow to Peking, and had finally arrived
too late.

A Socialist delegate told me how even the Ikeda Cabinet was split on the question of Japanese trade with China. On the one hand, certain die-hard anti-Communists believed that for political as well as for economic reasons Japan should not trade with Communist-bloc countries. Ikeda himself thought this way. On the other hand, there were those who, strongly nationalistic but not at all pro-Communist, felt that Japan owes no particular loyalty to the West, and that it should do business in accordance with its best interests. The Minister of Construction, Ichiro Kono, was of that opinion, and he was supported from outside the Cabinet by a former Cabinet member, Eisaku Sato. At the time this was written, it appeared that the pro-trade sentiment in Japan was gaining ground.

The visits of Japanese missions to Peking were followed with concern by Washington. In the autumn of 1962, it was not just delegations of Socialists and Communists (generally mixed), or peace groups, that were going to China. One group, which visited the capital at the invitation of Premier Chou En-lai, was composed of influential members of Japan's governing party, the Liberal Democrats (liberal in name and conservative in platform). Coinciding with the visit of this delegation, there was talk that Japan's ban on credit to China would be lifted if payment could be guaranteed by a "third country"—for example, Switzerland or England.

Japanese businessmen were irritated at the situation because, while they had for years abstained from trading with China in order not to expose themselves to reprisals by Americans, the latter were employing more or less clandestine methods to evade the laws of their own country.

As for the Japanese government, it was trying to solve the problem by relaxing its pressure on the businessmen, while at the same time pacifying Washington by insisting that any modification of its policy would be applied on an economic plane, not a political plane. But it was evident that the very act of entrusting to a state body the study and preparation of an agreement with Peking implied *de facto* recognition of China's Communist regime.

The Leaking Embargo

The absurdity of the attempted embargo against China was revealed clearly during our visit to the Peking Cancer Hospital, directed by our good friend, Professor Wu Huan-hsing.

When we first met Dr. Wu in 1957, he was directing the Shanghai Radiological Institute. We discovered immediately that we had friends in common. He had worked in his specialty in London until 1944. He told us then of the early accomplishments of China's Health Campaign, and in particular how opium addicts (now greatly diminished in number) were identified and taken to sanitoriums for treatment. He explained the methods that had been adopted to end the "work sickness" in the rice fields, a disease which had victimized so many in the past.

But what had impressed me most was Dr. Wu's story of his personal experience with the new regime. He had returned to China from London after the end of the Second World War, possessed with the desire to use what he had learned in England for the benefit of his country. So he sent the Chiang Kai-shek government a memorandum with a series of concrete proposals for the fight against cancer and for furthering medical research. This memorandum, and several subsequent ones, elicited no response from the authorities, and our friend was beginning to consider seriously one of the many tempting invitations he had received to work in other countries. But the change of regime in 1949 came in time to reward him for his patience and patriotism. The People's Republic offered him the means to do what he wanted to do. And in 1957 he had told us: "We are lucky enough to have at the head of the new regime a man full of imagination and understanding."

The allusion to Mao Tse-tung was made with conviction and sincerity, but delicately and with the explanation that, while Dr. Wu was not political, he was a Chinese patriot. He added: "If I had to produce 300 trained radiologists, all I would need to do would be to make a request to the government. Whether or not there was money for other things, I would receive all that I needed in the fight against cancer."

Now, in his new Peking hospital, Dr. Wu sought a special instrument produced in the United States. The hospital tried to buy one, but the embargo stood in the way: no medical instruments for China! Unable to purchase the instrument, the Chinese manufactured it themselves in Shanghai. Result: China had an instrument of its own manufacture—and a very good one, according to Dr. Wu—which was presently being exported to Asiatic and African countries at a price lower than that asked by the U.S. manufacturer.

The incident was more than a demonstration of the futility of the American embargo against China; it reflected badly on the United States, which had been shown up as wanting to deprive China of a weapon against one of mankind's dread scourges.

The Taiwan Question

I have personally never believed that the People's Republic would go to war over Taiwan (Formosa). For one thing, China's leaders are convinced that the island must inevitably return to its homeland in the natural course of events.

The British, even though the "elasticity" of their U.N. policy leads them to throw their vote with the Americans in support of Chiang Kai-shek, recognize clearly that Taiwan is an inseparable part of China. No one with the slightest respect for history can doubt it. In the year 607—more than 1,350 years ago—an emperor of the Sui dynasty dispatched an official to Taiwan to handle the island's administration.

In 1624 the Dutch, and subsequently the Portuguese, occupied part of Taiwan, but were dislodged by the Chinese in 1662. There was a period of Japanese rule after 1895, as a consequence of China's defeat in the Sino-Japanese war. But in 1943, in the Cairo Declaration, Britain and the United States declared that "all territories that Japan has stolen from the Chinese, such as Manchuria, Formosa, and the Pescadores, will be returned to the Republic of China." Accordingly, Japan returned Taiwan to China on October 25, 1945.

China and Spain

At the end of one of the state banquets to which we were invited, Premier Chou En-lai left his place at the head table and walked over to the table where my wife and I were seated with some Chinese friends. He came to drink a toast with us to the liberation of Spain. That gesture symbolized, for us, the attitude of the New China toward the struggle of the Spanish people to free themselves from their Fascist chains.

Days before the banquet, I had been received by Foreign Minister Chen Yi. It was, of course, not I personally who was so honored, but the cause I served; in giving me an audience, the Marshal was simply extending the hand of friendship to many, far away, who were struggling for freedom as his own people had been doing in the not too distant past.

My interview with the Foreign Minister was, I thought, a private affair, and I wrote nothing about it in the dispatches I was sending to my newspapers. But the next morning the Peking press published a story, with a photograph of Marshal Chen Yi saying goodby to us. The story was an eloquent sign of sympathy and support for the cause of the Spanish people.

The word "liberation" has a special meaning in China as a result of years of effort and struggle. When it is joined to the word "Spain," it acquires a peculiar importance. For solidarity with the Spanish people in their struggle for liberation has come to be part of China's policy.

I am not referring merely to that earlier period, during the Chinese resistance, when the Chinese who were fighting the Japanese included among their battle songs the famous ballad of the Spanish civil war, *Madrid*. The Madrid that we in Spain had sought to defend even after the fall of Catalonia had become for the Chinese fighters an inspiring symbol of resistance. In those days, Chinese units were frequently designated by the Spanish word *guerrillas* and these warriors, under the fire of Japanese aviation, would shout: "Let us resist like the Spaniards!"

All that is moving and unforgettable. But it is necessary to emphasize that China's feeling for the Spanish people has not changed. The fight in Spain, *today's* fight, finds a consistent and loyal ally in China. The sense of solidarity of the Chinese people for the people of Spain is supplemented by the political vision that China's leaders display in relation to our struggle. In the situation created by the world-wide contest between progress and reaction, as a consequence of the advance of socialism and the panic which that advance has caused, Spain has acquired a particular importance. For Spain is the country from which an effective challenge can be launched against the reactionary offensive sustained by nations which consider themselves strongholds of liberalism, but whose strategy leads them to salute Franco as their comrade-in-arms. The defeat of that offensive, on a world-wide scale, could best be advanced by the overthrow of the Franco dictatorship.

It is because Peking sees the Spanish problem in this broad perspective that the Spanish strikes in the spring of 1962 were greeted throughout China with such signs of enthusiasm. In the universities, the factories, the communes, resolutions by the thousands were approved acclaiming the miners in Asturias and the rest of Spain, the metal workers in the Basque country, the other striking workers of Catalonia and Madrid. As for the Chinese News Agency, whose English bulletins we continued to receive after we left China, it featured the Spanish strikes for many weeks.

The manifestations of sympathy for the Spanish cause to which I have referred were not the only ones I encountered. An extraordinarily well-informed audience attended a series of lectures I gave at the Institute of Foreign Affairs. Then, at the thoughtful initiative of the Institute, I gave a special lecture on Spain, in Spanish (an excellent Chinese translator was furnished); an unusually large and attentive audience was present, and at the end of my talk their questions showed how assiduously they had been following Spanish affairs.

In my visits to the Military Museum of the Chinese Revolution in Peking and the Museum of the Resistance in Shanghai, the association between the two struggles, China's and Spain's, was evident in the minds of the army officers who gave us explanations of the photographs, diagrams and documents on display.

One day at the Palace of Culture of the Shanghai workers,

I had a particularly illuminating conversation with a former Resistance leader, himself a worker. From him I heard a most impressive description of how, in a revolutionary struggle, a lack of material means can be offset by the possession of a clear political line and a determined leadership. He spoke colorfully of China's revolutionary tactics: of how strikes and mass protests were combined to combat rising prices or lack of food; how offensives launched at carefully selected spots were expanded to other favorable terrains; how bold blows were alternated with pauses used for reorganizing the revolutionary forces.

All this time China's oppressive regime, not satisfied with its numerically superior forces, had considerable foreign aid at its disposal. My worker friend recalled the presence of 50 foreign warships in Shanghai harbor. The fleet formed part of the government's tactic of intimidation; the object was to convince the Chinese workers and students, poorly armed and without financial resources, of the futility of their efforts. My friend showed us a proclamation, issued at the time by Mao Tse-tung, which advised the workers and students to "fight, fail, fight again, fail again, return to the fight—until victory is won!" Mao stressed the importance of actions, however small, that would produce practical results. The Chairman's philosophy in this regard is summed up in the title of one of his pamphlets: "One spark alone can start a prairie fire."

The Minister of Foreign Affairs

My interview with Foreign Minister Chen Yi was not limited to a discussion of the situation in Spain. In fact, the range of our conversation was world-wide.

Chen Yi described the governments of Burma, Cambodia, Nepal, Afghanistan, and Ceylon as following a correct policy of neutrality and peace and knowing how to maintain their national independence. He expressed approval of India's recovery of Goa as ending a foreign domination which had lasted more than four centuries—his country's differences with India over certain border territories notwithstanding.

The Arab world as a whole appears to him to be changing profoundly and developing favorably. But it was particularly for the people of Algeria, victorious at last in their struggle for independence, that the Marshal most eloquently expressed his nation's friendship. (That China's concern for Algeria and the Algerian liberation movement has consisted of more than mere eloquence was made clear by Captain Si Bahkhti of Algeria's National Liberation Army in a statement he made to the Associated Press a few days after his country achieved independence. "China saved our revolution, for which we are grateful to her," he said. He went on to explain that when, in 1960, the nationalist movement found itself unable to obtain aid of any kind from the West, it turned Eastward and found the hand of friendship. "Mao," said Captain Bahkhti, "gave us $150 million. He also increased facilities for training our aviators in various Moslem countries. Thanks in great part to the aid provided by the Chinese communists, the N.L.A. has weapons today for an army of 300,000 men.")

China's Minister of Foreign Affairs also showed a lively interest in what is taking place in Latin America. All in all, the peoples of Asia, Africa, and Latin America are regarded by him in terms of a community of purpose and of frank solidarity.

Chen Yi's participation in the Geneva conference on Laos offered an opportunity to Western observers to appreciate the diplomatic qualities of China's foreign minister. They found him candid in his exposition of his country's foreign policies. He did not hide the fact that one of the goals of that policy was to aid all countries struggling to free themselves from imperialism. Chen Yi predicted that the people of Laos would be victorious, despite all intrigues and delaying tactics, and he viewed with optimism future developments in the rest of Asia, including Japan.

Chen Yi has confidence in the Japanese people. He is aware of the powerful influence on Japan that America continues to exercise, but he is encouraged by the opposition to Washington shown by the working class, the students, and the Japanese peace movement.

Concerning South Korea, he said that the people who ended the rule of Syngman Rhee will also end the rule of "the other Syngman Rhees" who have succeeded him. And as for the South Vietnam despotism, he considered it doomed to fall. In the meantime, he foresaw a succession of war-lords ruling the country who would be interested only in receiving American aid, not in the "democratic reforms" that the United States would like to see adopted in order to prolong its influence in a region that has become one of its chief bases of military operations in Asia.

China is carrying out a systematic educational effort throughout Asia. At the Eighth World Conference Against Atomic and Hydrogen Bombs, which met in Tokyo in August of 1962, Pa Chin, head of the Chinese delegation, reiterated the principles and goals of the People's Republic. "The People's Republic," he said then, "is too familiar with the horrors of war to desire another one. We have suffered a great deal from aggression and that is why we are completely identified with the struggles for independence and liberation of other peoples. We will certainly not take a single inch of territory which belongs to others, but on the other hand we will not permit a single inch of our territory to be taken from us by force."

Relations with Africa

For some years now, two Chinese organizations have been operating in the field of Afro-Asian relations: the Committee for Afro-Asiatic Solidarity and the Society for Sino-African Friendship. There can be no clearer proof of the depth of China's interest in Africa than that recently a third organization has been created, the Afro-Asiatic Society. The new group is designed to serve as an intellectual bridge between the New China and Africa's emerging nations, and has been entrusted with the administration of an ambitious cultural exchange program. As this is written, the Society was planning the establishment of a university in Peking for African and Asiatic students, similar to the Patrice Lumumba University the Russians established in Moscow. (We had spent a very agreeable evening, while in Moscow, talking to the students of that university; among them we had found many Latin Americans.)

The president of the new Society is Chou Yang, formerly one of Chairman Mao's close collaborators and, until 1955, the Vice Minister of Cultural Affairs. Of the new organization's four Vice Presidents, three belong to one or the other of the democratic parties and have distinguished themselves in the study of African and Asiatic affairs. Its roster of professors and advisers includes the most respected names among the Chinese intelligentsia. Some are non-party people—a fact indicating China's awareness of the variety of political systems and philosophies to be found in Africa.

In the field of trade, the People's Republic has established a basis for the closer cooperation it hopes to develop in coming years. In 1959 a trade agreement was signed by China and Morocco for the first time. It provided for 57 million dirhams ($11.4 million) worth of products to be exchanged for the period 1959-1960. Since then, the agreement has been renewed several times.

China concluded two agreements with Guinea, one for trade and another for technical and economic cooperation, in 1960 on the occasion of President Sékou Touré's visit to Peking. Valid for five years, the agreement provided for an annual exchange of goods amounting to 1,200 million Guinean francs ($348 million). Guinea is supplying coffee, industrial diamonds, palm oil, and other products; in return, China is exporting rice, fabrics, agricultural machinery, office supplies, pharmaceuticals and other items.

The signing of similar agreements between Ghana and China coincided with President Nkrumah's visit to Peking, which took place while we were there. These agreements involved the exchange of about $19 million in products for the first year. To facilitate this exchange, Peking offered the Accra government an interest-free loan of some $17 million, repayable in ten annual installments beginning in 1971.

With Mali a trade agreement was accompanied by economic and technical cooperation. A Chinese mission went to Bamako to study the possibility of introducing the cultivation of tea and sugar in the Sikasso region. A similar trade and technical mission was planned for Algeria.

True, the volume of trade and the number of technical agreements concluded so far between China and the new nations of Africa have not yet reached large proportions. Equally true, not all of these agreements have yet been completely fulfilled, either because of temporary economic conditions in China or because of unexpected situations arising in this or that signatory country. But all of this, in my opinion, is secondary to the important fact that China has a well-considered African policy that combines immediate with potential possibilities, and is based on the great attraction that China unquestionably exerts on the undeveloped countries.

The methods used by such Western institutions as the Investment Fund for Economic and Social Development have proved inadequate to meet the needs of these young countries. They suffer from miscalculations in the planning of social investments; they are frequently useless as far as infrastructure expenditures are concerned; and the funds made available are sometimes employed in spectacular projects which serve only to mask a simple transfer of colonial domination from one country to another.

China has more practical things to offer the emerging nations, as the numerous African delegations we met in Peking and the provinces have been able to see for themselves. Mao Tse-tung always finds time to receive these visitors, many of whom have told me they were greatly impressed by the Chairman's knowledge of, and objective approach to, their problems. Instead of recommending to them what might be termed maximum-type programs, Mao stresses the advisability of gradual, patient efforts, with immediate goals adjusted to the conditions, as well as the needs, of each individual country. For some of the delegates, unfamiliar with the Chinese way of harmonizing firmness in doctrine with flexibility in application, it is a surprise to hear him talking like this.

The best publicized of Mao's interviews with visiting Africans took place during May and June, 1960; a small book has been written about them. These talks set the pattern for China's policies toward the new African states and their problems—policies which the Africans describe as generous and altogether free of opportunism.

In Hangchow, on April 28, 1961, Chairman Mao expressed to a group of African leaders his confidence in the future of their nations. This moment in history, he told them, favored the African peoples. They could, he went on, thwart all attempts to supplant the old colonialism with other forms of domination by extending the basis of their national revolutions as widely as possible—that is, uniting their workers, peasants, intellectuals, and all other anti-colonial elements in support of a clearly determined political line.

At a dinner honoring President Nkrumah of Ghana in August, 1961, Liu Shao-chi, China's President, declared that the awakening of the African peoples was one of the great events of the century. African unity, he said, was the answer to all forms of neo-colonialism. The movement toward African unity, he added, was followed in China with the deepest approval and the greatest hope.

Premier Chou En-lai, speaking at a reception in the Congo Embassy on June 29, 1961, denounced Western policy in the Congo. He exalted the figure of Lumumba, and insisted that all colonial forces should leave the Congo. "Even though China and the Congo are separated by great oceans and thousands of miles," he continued, "their common struggle against imperialism and colonialism has united the two peoples."

China's leaders reject the widely held view that the independent African nations are incapable of solving their national problems. They believe that an independent Africa will find its own road and that the duty of the socialist countries is to aid the Africans to find that road, whether the great powers like it or not.

This long-range attitude of China with relation to Africa produced a warm response in the African countries, according to many African visitors to Peking whom I met. I found further proof of Africa's interest in preserving China's friendship when, as a journalist, I covered the fall, 1962, session of the General Assembly in New York. At that session I witnessed a maneuver by certain Western delegations designed to turn the Afro-Asian bloc against China when the Sino-Indian controversy came up on the agenda. The maneuver failed—and so did several others to the same purpose. The African delegations' reluctance to join the anti-Chinese campaign was strengthened when Peking announced a cease-fire in the border war, and began to withdraw its troops at a time when they had been advancing almost without opposition. "After all," certain African delegates were heard to say, "China is the victor and she voluntarily withdraws her troops and offers to negotiate. What more does India want?"

A letter on the Sino-Indian dispute published in *The New York Times* of November 11, 1962, made a strong impression on the African delegates. The letter was signed by two prominent Chinese, former members of the Chiang Kai-shek government, and still clearly out of sympathy with the communist regime in Peking. Nevertheless the two men—one of them a professor at Fairleigh Dickinson University in New Jersey—wrote that "no Chinese, regardless of political beliefs, will ever subscribe to the validity of the so-called McMahon Line" on which India based its border claims. The writers continued:

The government in Taiwan has expressed the sentiment of all Chinese in its statement of October 30. Bitter as it is against communism, it is at one with the Chinese communist government on this matter. "The so-called McMahon Line," it said, "is a line unilaterally claimed by the British during their rule over India. The Government of the Republic of China [Formosa's Nationalist regime] has never accepted this line of demarcation. . . ." It is scarcely necessary to say that until the validity of this hypothetical boundary line is established, there will always be friction between India and her northern neighbor, whether that neighbor is governed by the communists or by any other Chinese government.

China's satisfactory treaty with Nepal, fixing the borders between the two countries, and the fact that in the midst of the Sino-Indian hostilities tiny Butan remained calm and unafraid that the Chinese might invade its territory, also contributed to the conviction of the Afro-Asian bloc in the U.N. that India ought to accept the Peking government's proposal to negotiate.

By all accounts, the courtesies extended to Africans in China were repaid when Chinese delegations visited Africa. One Chinese delegation, returning from Mali, told how leaders from the interior of that country had come some 15 miles on horseback to greet them. Another delegation, returned from Guinea, had been bidden farewell with these words: "When the Guinean people have 650 million Chinese friends, what do the imperialists matter?"

All other nations now competing for the friendship of Africa, an Africa that one day will constitute a formidable factor in the complex of world forces, are going to find a first-class rival in the New China. One African delegate whom I met in China told me:

"In Africa, our main inspiration is the Chinese idea. The United States and the Soviet Union set examples beyond the reach of our means. Not so China. Here we are learning how one can advance with the little one has available. The progressive intellectuals in Africa—and in Latin America, too, judging from what I have heard—feel that the Chinese model is best for us: its accelerated development in agriculture and industry, the massive mobilization of its citizens to achieve concrete goals, the enthusiastic popular support of the political line drawn by the leaders."

I also met in Peking a lieutenant of Lumumba, who escaped his chief's fate by no more than an eyelash. He told me: "There is certainly one country that helps with no other motive than that of aiding those who are fighting for liberation, and that country is China."

One of the things that most surprises China's neighbors is the continuity of its policy of solidarity with the underdeveloped countries. This line was followed even through the years of natural disasters, when China suffered painful privations at home. China's foreign-aid commitments approached the figure of $250 million, distributed among different neutralist countries: Burma, Cambodia, Ceylon, Indonesia, Nepal, Morocco, Guinea, and Ghana, aside from its aid to Cuba. In most cases, loans were extended without interest.

Main Lines of Policy

A communique distributed by the New China News Agency on September 28, 1962, shortly after a meeting of the Central Committee of the Chinese Communist Party, described the General Line of Chinese foreign policy as follows:

(1) Development of friendship, mutual aid, and cooperation with the Soviet Union and other fraternal Socialist countries in accord with the principles of proletarian internationalism.

(2) Establishment of peaceful coexistence on the basis of the "five principles" with countries of different social systems.

(3) Opposition to the war-like policies of the imperialists.

(4) Assistance to the revolutionary struggles of the oppressed nations against imperialism and colonialism.

Compare this statement of general principles, made in the autumn of 1962, with my interview with Premier Chou in the spring of 1957, and the continuity of Chinese policy will be seen. Nor has this policy changed fundamentally in any way since 1962.

Chinese foreign policy combines firmness and *souplesse*—the French word that, better than any other, expresses a readiness to avoid unnecessary harshness and a determination never to confuse desire with reality. It is a profoundly realistic policy.

9

CHINA AND RUSSIA

Despite all that has been said in this book about the Western tendency to underestimate China, the West really is perfectly aware of what is happening in that country. The truth is that the West fears China. This being so, how natural that Western political strategists should speculate on a worsening of relations between Peking and Moscow, forecasting a future in which the West need no longer worry about the spectacle of two great powers marching together toward a single goal.

At the outset, the Sino-Soviet controversy developed in a relatively tranquil manner. My experiences in China encouraged me to think that it might continue in this fashion; all the time I was there I heard not a single word of criticism of the Soviet Union. On the contrary, many times I was told by the Chinese, as they showed me some of their achievements, "We were helped a great deal in this undertaking by our Soviet comrades." Nevertheless, as was revealed later, differences between the two countries had already grown quite sharp.

Soviet Premier Khrushchev's first savage attack on Stalin came at the Twentieth Congress of the Soviet Communist Party, in 1956. At no point did China participate in the anti-Stalinist campaign that followed. In the 1957 May Day parade in Peking, Stalin's portrait, together with those of Marx, Engels, Lenin, and Mao Tse-tung, was in its usual place of honor. It occupied the same place in 1961 and 1962. Only a few days before Stalin's remains were removed from Red Square in Moscow, Chou En-lai had placed a wreath upon it.

In a lengthy analysis of the Stalin era printed in *Jenmin Jih Pao* (*The People's Daily*), emphasis was placed on the need to keep attacks on Stalin from being used by the Right to attack communism. In the opinion of the Peking leaders, comments on the Stalin era ought to take account of its accomplishments as well as its failures.

The Chinese leaders regarded the issues raised at the Twentieth Congress as consistent with their theoretical position on "contradictions." To them, denial of the existence of contradictions within the framework of Marxism amounted to a denial of dialectics. From their point of view, contradiction between what is individual and what is collective in a socialist society is inevitable.

I happened to be in Peking in 1957 when Mao Tse-tung issued a long statement on that very question. Accepting the fact that contradictions within the movement were inevitable, Mao argued only that the debates attending them ought to be held within reasonable limits. He argued that the points at issue did not represent a "fundamental conflict of interests"; they were, he said, not "basic." Rather, said Mao, the contradictions represented an encounter between "correct and erroneous opinions."

Reaction to the Sputnik

One of the "contradictions" was revealed in China's reaction to the communique carried by Tass on August 26, 1957, announcing that the Soviet Union had successfully tested an intercontinental ballistic missile. There followed, on October 4 and November 3, news of the launching of the Soviet Union's first two earth satellites.

Khrushchev called these achievements of Soviet science a step toward acquisition of the "ultimate weapon," and both capitals—Peking and Moscow—emphasized that these events had automatically produced a profound alteration in the balance of world forces.

From a study of the post-Sputnik press in the Soviet Union, it is apparent that the Russians saw their achievement chiefly in the light of the deterrent effect it would have on those in the United States who had been advocating preventive war. In October of 1958, Khrushchev said that the situation was such that the West would "hardly dare to unleash a war against the countries of the socialist camp."

Commentaries in the Chinese press at that time placed

emphasis less on the element of deterrence than on the "qualitative change in the distribution of world power" which had occurred. The phrase "paper tiger," reserved for American imperialism, expressed the concept—i.e., that the West had suddenly found its "position of strength" policy reduced to a pretense.

In February, 1958, Chou En-lai stressed, in a speech, the "decisive change" which he said had taken place in the international situation as a result of the Soviet achievements. "The socialist camp," he said, "is winning supremacy in population and popular support." The imperialists themselves, he insisted, realize that they are facing an "invincible" socialist coalition led by the Soviet Union.

The Split Widens

On the other hand, Khrushchev—to judge by his statements and the contemporary Soviet press—appeared to prefer to use his nation's enhanced power to further the idea of negotiation. In his opinion, the Sputnik should give socialist diplomacy needed flexibility in its search for a common ground on which East and West might achieve a lessening of tensions. He believed this to be possible and was prepared to devote himself to the task with all the impetus of his extraordinary personality.

Various events since that time, such as the Middle East crisis in the summer of 1958, revealed growing differences between Peking and Moscow in how best to use the shift in world power relations to check the promoters of dangerous international incidents. A case in point was the United States and British military landings in Lebanon and Jordan following the anti-Western coup in Iraq. The landings pointed to a possible further development: active Western intervention against Iraq. An editorial in *Jenmin Jih Pao* warned: "Nothing can be saved by giving in to evil." It insisted that the imperialists were always very fierce with the weak, but feared the strong. In contrast, a *Pravda* editorial, while affirming that the USSR could not remain indifferent in the face of what was happening near its borders, called for reason and calm, taking into account that the United States as well as the Soviet Union possessed nuclear weapons.

Similar differences in the approach of the two Communist powers were revealed when plans for a visit by the Soviet Premier to Washington were announced. The Chinese press showed itself far more skeptical than the Russian press about the possibility of achieving practical results from the confrontation. I went to Washington to cover this important event, and found American left-wingers thoroughly convinced that the Premier's talks with President Eisenhower would have considerable influence on American foreign policy. This was not at all the Chinese position. China's Foreign Minister, Chen Yi, speaking at an Indonesian reception in Peking, warned that the imperialists "would never renounce by their own free will their policy of war and aggression."

The failure of the Summit Conference in Paris, in part as a consequence of the U-2 incident, resulted in a still wider division between Moscow and Peking over the policy to be followed by the Communist bloc in its relations with the West, and in particular with the United States.

The Twenty-First Congress

The Twenty-First Congress of the Communist Party of the USSR, although it received less attention than either its predecessor or successor, was none the less important. It provided the occasion for Khrushchev to take a stand on some of the points that China and Russia had been debating. His pronouncement threw a clear light on the issue of the *détente,* that is, on the possibility of an agreement that would lessen international tensions.

In the Soviet Premier's view, the *détente* not only served the cause of peace, but was almost indispensable for solidifying and consolidating the communist bloc. The fundamental problem for the next seven years, he said, is to win as much ground as possible in the economic competition between socialism and capitalism. To achieve a clear advantage over capitalism would have a profound influence on the international situation; it would attract millions of new partisans to the camp of socialism and thus lead to a strengthening of the forces of peace; it would bring about great changes not only within the USSR, but everywhere; it would mean a world-wide shift toward socialism.

The Soviet Premier's thesis can be summed up as follows: The reality of the progress made by the USSR and its allies ought to convince even the most extreme imperialists of the futility of unleashing a war against the socialist coalition. In fact, Khrushchev posited "a real possibility of excluding world war from the life of society even before the complete triumph of socialism."

Relations with Kennedy

The accession of John F. Kennedy to the Presidency of the United States accentuated the discrepancy between Moscow and Peking in judging American political developments. Peking did not share the confidence bestowed on Kennedy as the promoter of peace by a vast sector of the Left in many parts of the world. Questions raised by a few who had followed the new President's career closely, and who doubted the public image of him as a man of peace, were met with visible irritation. For many, of course, that image was shattered with the American action against Cuba in 1961. But the Cuban affair was soon relegated to the background.

A few days after the U.N. Assembly met that year, there again prevailed widespread confidence that a Kennedy-Khrushchev meeting would lead to an agreement on Berlin and assure a long period of world peace. This persisted until October 22, when the declaration of the U.S. blockade of Cuba, and the terms in which it was announced by President Kennedy, put an end to the illusions that had been maintained. But the Chinese had continued all along to express skepticism, and when the great shock to world opinion took place over the measures adopted by Kennedy against Cuba, Peking could say, "I told you so."

Sino-Soviet Meeting in Moscow

This record of shifting events and attitudes brings us to July 5, 1963, when the Chinese and Soviet delegations met in Moscow with Teng Hsiao-ping and Suslov presiding. The meeting sharpened, rather than blunted, the points of difference. In line with their view that it was better for everything to be revealed and discussed, the Chinese leaders expressed satisfaction that the divergent theses would finally come into the open. Two lengthy documents presented the theses of both sides in complete detail: the letter of the Chinese Communist Party dated June 14, 1963, and the Soviet reply dated July 14. These two documents, which have been published and widely circulated in many languages, constitute the basis for an objective study of the Sino-Soviet controversy, and I refer the reader to them.

It is evident from this conflict of ideas that the Chinese Communist Party opposes the concentration of socialist-bloc foreign policy on "peaceful coexistence" as defined and practiced by the Soviet Union during the last few years. The Chinese thesis clearly established that, "like the USSR of Lenin," the Chinese People's Republic has "practiced with firmness and consistency this policy of peaceful coexistence." But then the Chinese go on to emphasize that to restrict the platform of the international communist movement to "peaceful coexistence," or "peaceful competition," or "peaceful transition," is to renounce the historic mission of the proletarian revolution.

The Soviet position insisted, above all, that "the Chinese comrades clearly underestimate the danger of a thermonuclear war" and that the rockets and other atomic arms developed since the middle of the century have made obsolete the old conceptions of armed conflict.

This point is of capital importance, since the way in which it was developed and publicized was to influence powerfully the attitude not only of the various communist parties, but also leftist and pacifist opinion and the attitude of the public in general. To present China as being in favor of a thermonuclear war, or as playing recklessly with nuclear "brinkmanship," while picturing the Soviet Union as willing to make concessions to the West to avoid such a war, was to assure beforehand that the reaction against China would be overwhelming, at least for the time being. It appealed to the people's deep desire to see humanity free of the threat of nuclear war. It surrounded China with an atmosphere of hostility.

Peking energetically rejected the Soviet accusation. As the reader can see from the evidence presented in this book, to represent Peking as counting the days until it has its own bomb to hurl at the rest of the world is quite contrary to the facts. The only statement Mao Tse-tung released for publication after his long talk with Edgar Snow a couple of years ago was this: "We do not want war. We hold that war should not be used as a means to settle disputes between nations." On other occasions, while discussing the subject of war with foreign visitors, Mao commented that if he thought he could induce the imperialists to refrain from nuclear warfare by showing fear of it, he would tell the Chinese to be very much afraid; but he feels that this would provoke rather than deter an imperialist attack.

Nevertheless, China continued to be accused of wanting war. In order to substantiate the charge, it was often accompanied by "evidence" fabricated to fill the need for facts. During the summer of 1963, and more particularly following China's incessant criticism of the Moscow Treaty for the partial banning of nuclear tests, a great deal was written and said about a new Chinese assault on India. It meant nothing that, even from New Delhi, Western diplomatic observers expressed the opinion that the sensational reports about Chinese troop movements on the Indian border were based on evidence that was only hearsay.

What is certain is that Peking disputes the effectiveness of peaceful coexistence, as it is practiced today by Moscow, in checking the forces of aggression. It is also true that from the very first, Peking underlined the extent of the concessions that would have to be made to reach an understanding with the Americans. The Chinese accused the United States of wanting only to gain time for its aggressive plans against the revolutionary movements.

The Test-Ban Treaty

In the midst of the jubilation which greeted the test-ban treaty in Moscow, Washington, London, and elsewhere, by the Right as well as the Left, the cold voice of Peking was heard declining any part of the celebration. Aside from emphasizing the limited nature of the agreement and the concession made by

Khrushchev in renouncing his original demand for a non-aggression agreement between the Warsaw Pact and NATO countries, Peking made the following points:

(1) The three nuclear powers that signed the treaty were seeking merely to consolidate their nuclear monopoly and tie the hands of all countries that want peace and are the victims of the nuclear menace. China opposes the idea of a super-directorate of two, the United States and the Soviet Union, taking control of the world and dividing the zones of influence between them; opposition to this idea is constantly stressed in the Chinese criticism of Moscow's policy.

(2) The world's peoples are asking for a true peace; this treaty gives them only a fictitious one that deceives the world into believing that the danger of a nuclear holocaust has disappeared. The Chinese government declines to be a party to so dangerous a mystification.

(3) The Moscow treaty separates the questions of banning nuclear *tests* and banning nuclear *arms*. Peking maintains that legalizing the continued manufacture of weapons of mass destruction, their stockpiling, and their use by the three nuclear powers are all diametrically opposed to the concept of disarmament.

(4) As long as military research continues to develop weapons of destruction not covered by the Moscow treaty, the danger of war exists. But the artificial enthusiasm aroused among the peoples of the world by the combined campaigns of the Soviet and Western press around the Moscow Treaty paralyzes the forces of peace.

In developing the fourth point, the *People's Daily* of Peking insisted that the treaty, far from serving the cause of peace, weakens it by throwing sand into people's eyes. The editorial made the point that it was natural for the Western imperialists to be overjoyed at the signing of the treaty; what was surprising was the rejoicing in the socialist camp.

While talk of the Moscow Treaty was making headlines, Peking proposed that an international conference be convoked for the purpose of banning nuclear arms altogether. Since the proposal constitutes an important element in the Great Debate, I reproduce it here in its original terms:

(1) All countries in the world, both nuclear and non-nuclear, solemnly declare that they will prohibit and destroy nuclear weapons completely, thoroughly, totally, and resolutely. Concretely speaking, they will not use nuclear weapons, nor export, nor import, nor manufacture, nor test, nor stockpile them; and they will destroy all the existing nuclear weapons and their means of delivery in the world, and disband all existing establishments for the research, testing, and manufacture of nuclear weapons in the world.

(2) In order to fulfill the above undertakings step by step, the following measures shall be adopted:

    (a) Dismantle all military bases, including nuclear bases, on foreign soil, and withdraw from abroad all nuclear weapons and their means of delivery.

    (b) Establish a nuclear-weapon-free zone of the Asian and Pacific region, including the United States, the Soviet Union, China, and Japan; a nuclear-weapon-free zone of Central Europe; a nuclear-weapon-free zone of Africa; and a nuclear-weapon-free zone of Latin America. The countries possessing nuclear weapons shall undertake due obligations with regard to each of the nuclear-weapon-free zones.

    (c) Refrain from exporting and importing in any form nuclear weapons and technical data for their manufacture.

    (d) Cease all nuclear tests, including underground nuclear tests.

(3) A conference of the government heads of all the countries of the world shall be convened to discuss the question of the prohibition and thorough destruction of nuclear weapons and the question of taking the above-mentioned four measures in order to realize step by step the complete prohibition and thorough destruction of nuclear weapons.

Upon publication of the proposal, the Norwegian government promptly suggested that the doors of the U.N. be opened to Peking to allow for full-dress debate on it.

The fact is that the Asiatic continent, on which China's influence will increase in the years to come, can no longer be left on the fringe of great decisions. To demand China's mechanical and routine support of a certain kind of "peaceful coexistence," in the effectiveness of which it does not believe, is to approach the general problem of disarmament in too narrow a fashion.

Leftists who take an anti-Chinese position must sometimes find it difficult to justify their stance. What can one say, for instance, about the Stewart Alsop article which appeared in the *Saturday Evening Post* of September 28, 1963, under the significant title, "The Real Meaning of the Test Ban"? Wrote Mr. Alsop:

"In the collective judgment of the President [Kennedy] and his chief advisers, the Chinese Communists simply cannot be permitted to achieve [nuclear] power. . . . Thanks to the U-2s and to other secret devices, the intelligence community knows precisely where the two main Chinese atomic plants are. Such plants are highly vulnerable to even a single high-explosive bomb. The 'nuclear sterilization' of China is thus technically an easy problem."

In short, Alsop projects a full-fledged plan for the nuclear bombardment of China in the name of peace. Mr. Alsop is not the government of the United States, but it is generally accepted that he was very close to the White House during the Kennedy administration.

Wars of Liberation

China's criticism of "the new era of peace," Khrushchev style, was extended to the issue of peoples' struggles for liberation. The apparent lessening in international tensions, the Chinese charged, was accomplished at the cost of liberation movements. No one must move a finger anywhere if this might disturb the Soviet-American idyll, caustically remarked a Peking commentator.

To all this, *Izvestia* replied that Peking was substituting the three A's—Asia, Africa and Latin America—for Marxism-Leninism, subtly imputing a racist attitude to the Chinese. (Spaniards opposing the Fascist dictatorship in Madrid think that *Izvestia* could well have added Spain to the list, for they fear that a Soviet-American rapprochement might easily extend peaceful coexistence to Franco.)

Maintaining Relations

In recent months, criticism of China by the USSR and those who support Moscow against Peking has become more acute. Not only is China's foreign policy attacked, but also its domestic accomplishments, especially the communes. And the Chinese, for their part, have not softened their criticism of the Soviet leaders. The Kremlin's proposal for a meeting of the communist parties throughout the world was rejected by Peking. "We shall see in four or five years," was the somewhat humorous reply of the *People's Daily*. In this connection, it is noteworthy that even several of the European communist parties, which are presumably closest to the Kremlin, have been reluctant to support Moscow's demand for an international "showdown," fearing that the result might be an irreparable split in the communist movement.

Despite growing strains, certain ties still seemed to bind the two countries together. In an interview with a Japanese news agency on May 17, 1964, Chou En-lai recognized the deterioration in relations but emphatically repeated that China would fight on the side of the USSR if the latter fell victim to "imperialist aggression." At the same time, the Chinese Premier again demonstrated the flexibility of his country's policies, declaring that the situation in Formosa might change and cooperation between Chinese Communists and Nationalists be made possible. He recalled that the United States had withdrawn its support of the Diem regime in South Vietnam and that it might do the same with Chiang Kai-shek.

A week prior to this interview, Foreign Minister Chen Yi talked to Claude Julien of *Le Monde*. Asked about China's nuclear future, Chen Yi replied:

"Our present industrial level allows us to advance in the field of nuclear exploration. It is not so difficult. The explosion of a nuclear weapon will take place when the exploratory work is finished. Our government, however, does not plan its foreign policy on the basis of whether or not we possess nuclear weapons. Some people think that China with atomic weapons will become arrogant. This is wrong. Others think that China without atomic weapons is weak. That is equally wrong."

The Foreign Minister went on to make a discreet reference

to the Sino-Soviet dispute: "We do not wish any countries to be our satellites, nor do we choose to be the satellite of another nation." Later, he noted: "I can announce to you officially that by the end of next year we shall have paid all our debts to the USSR. We owe the Soviet Union 5,600 million yuan, that is, about $2,400 million."

In the midst of charges and counter-charges, Peking and Moscow signed a trade agreement on May 13, 1964, which called upon China to pay its debt to the USSR before the stipulated expiration dates, and to deliver to the Russians metals and minerals, as well as chemical products, frozen pork, dairy products and textiles. The Soviet Union, in turn, will ship to China machinery, tractors, IL-18 transport planes, trucks, petroleum products and other items.

Summarizing the Dispute

From among the millions of words which have been written on the Sino-Soviet dispute, it may be helpful to summarize the essential points on which the two great Communist powers disagree.

On the Russian side, the main charge is that China wants war. Mikhail Suslov, chief Soviet theoretician, addressing the French Communist Party on May 15, 1964, declared that the Chinese "have contempt for the peace struggle. . . . In effect, they spur on the nuclear arms race."

The warmongering charge has been strenuously and repeatedly denied, publicly and privately, by both Chairman Mao and Premier Chou. Speaking at the celebration of the anniversary of the Chinese Revolution on October 1, 1963, Peng Chen, Mayor of Peking, who is also a leading member of the Chinese Communist Party's Politburo, energetically affirmed that "world peace can be preserved and the future of mankind can be infinitely bright."

Shortly after de Gaulle's recognition of Peking, the whole problem of China's attitude toward nuclear war came into sharp focus during an interview that Premier Chou En-lai gave to a representative of the French news agency. I give herewith the core of the exchange:

Question: "Is it true that in the event of a nuclear war China feels it is less vulnerable than any other country on the globe and that it could hope to emerge victorious from such a war, which might well destroy the rest of the world?"

Answer: "This is fabrication, pure and simple. Of every four persons in the world, one is Chinese. In a nuclear war, China would lose more people than other countries. The Chinese, like the French and other peoples of the world, resolutely oppose nuclear war. It is with ulterior motives that imperialists and certain others have unscrupulously distorted the position of China and made enormous propaganda out of the distortion. The Chinese government has consistently stood for the complete prohibition and total destruction of nuclear weapons and has proposed that a conference of heads of governments of all countries of the world should be convened to discuss the problem."

There is no doubt that the charge of "warmongering" against China has had a widespread effect. The majority of the people of the world do not understand much about the ideological or theoretical aspects of the Sino-Soviet dispute. But when they hear that the Russians want to protect them from atomic war, while the Chinese seek to drag them into one, their reaction is inevitable.

The chief accusations leveled against Moscow by the Chinese are (1) capitulation to the West and (2) failure to provide real support for the liberation movements whenever support might interfere with "peaceful coexistence."

The Chinese, who never believed Kennedy was a man of peace, have even less faith in President Johnson. They point to Vietnam, Laos, Cuba, and other world trouble spots. And they believe that a Johnson elected to a full four-year term in November, 1964, will be less a man of peace than was the Johnson who was President *pro tem*.

As has been intimated, the Moscow-Peking strains have reacted on other communist parties. The Communist Party of Romania, in the summer of 1964, was maintaining a strict neutrality in the dispute. The Polish and Italian parties, while officially favoring Moscow, were opposed to the Kremlin's call for a "showdown" meeting. The fact seems to be that the possibility of a definite and irreparable break between China and the USSR is frightening to many communists, socialists, progressives, and pacifists.

Events as they unfold will decide the issue. Meantime, Peking can smile at a situation which, by the end of May, 1964, saw the United States, still adamant in its refusal to recognize China, "expressing the hope"—to use the words of Robert J. McCloskey, State Department spokesman—"that those governments with which we have consulted on Laos and which have representatives in Peking would do what they could" to obtain China's assistance in halting the fight in that area.

10

DEMOCRACY AT WORK

The Minister of Education

During our second trip to China we made a point of visiting universities, special institutes, and schools to find out everything we could about the progress education has made in the five-year interval since our first visit. This inquiry ended with a long conversation with Liu Chih-yu, Minister of Education.

"To appreciate what has been done and what remains to be done in the field of education," the Minister began, "it is necessary to remember that in China two contradictory situations existed before the Liberation: on the one hand, we were a country of an ancient culture; on the other, we had an illiteracy rate of 95 percent, the result of a total lack of popular education.

"Not only were the people untaught, but no one had felt the necessity of teaching them. Until 1949 the vast majority of boys and girls grew up without schools, which were accessible only to the children of the rich. As for the national minorities, if some of them, such as the Koreans, were more advanced than others, in general it can be said that their educational level was almost rock bottom.

"In thirteen years of the People's Republic, the number of students has increased five times and, in some categories, far more. In 1949, there were 155,000 students in institutes of higher learning; today there are more than 800,000. Secondary-school attendance has increased from 1,870,000 to 12 million; that of primary schools, from 23 million to 90 million. The kindergartens have shown the most sensational increase: from 130,000 to 31 million.

"These figures give only a partial idea of what has been accomplished. One must add the number that attend classes organized for workers. At present, about 30 million workers study in their free time. Of these, more than 20 million attend part-time courses on the level of those taught in universities and institutes. So solid a basis has been laid that in the next few years China will have at its disposal far greater cadres of professionals and technicians than our Five-Year Plans had called for.

"We have proceeded by stages," the Minister continued. "From 1949 to 1952, we planned and accomplished the first advance in education. We began by utilizing everything available, improving where we could, at the same time ridding education of its privileged character. We wanted, not schools for the rich, but schools for the people.

"We had to create a new type of teacher, not by eliminating those already employed, but by trying to free them from the influence of a past dominated by imperialism and colonialism. You must know that in pre-Liberation China many intellectuals tended to regard themselves as servants and looked upon existing class and national differences as unalterable.

"During this first stage, we seized the schools supported by the Kuomintang and reformed them ideologically, beginning by eliminating fascist-type methods of pedagogy. We weeded out the foreign or 'foreignized' teachers whose retention would have meant exposing the new educational system to sabotage. At the time of Liberation, 21 of our universities, 500 secondary schools, 1,000 primary schools—comprising in all 360,000 teachers and students—were directed by foreigners, particularly Americans.

"To end all this was not simple. Even sympathizers of the Revolution held that it would be an error, considering the backwardness of China, to eliminate foreign teaching personnel when we still did not have sufficient teachers of our own.

"We introduced a new pedagogical system based on a double principle: education should promote national feeling and it should be open to all."

The Education Minister, at this point, provided me with the following outline describing the set-up of China's educational system as it operates today:

(1) *Full-time schools,* subdivided into:

    (a) Kindergartens for children of three to six years.

(b) Primary schools which provide a six-year program of studies.

(c) Secondary schools of the first cycle which generally provide a three-year program of studies, though in certain primary professional schools the duration of the study program varies.

(d) Secondary schools of the second cycle which provide another three-year program, with the exception of the secondary professional schools of technology, agronomy, pedagogy, general culture and public health, in which the courses may last four years.

(e) Schools of higher education wherein most courses of study last four years. Some courses—medicine, for example—last from five to six years.

(2) *Part-time schools.* This system, which has grown stupendously since 1958, was specifically designed to "put education at the service of the proletariat" and to "combine education and productive labor." For example, students of the secondary schools of agriculture work in the fields during the season of greatest agricultural activity, and study during the season when activity in the fields dwindles.

(3) *Adult Education.* These schools were organized for people who want to use their free time to improve their general education.

With respect to the adult education courses, the Education Minister had some explanatory remarks:

"It was absolutely necessary to promote the education of the adult population. We met this problem by establishing special courses that permitted attendance by adults engaged in other occupations, taking into account especially those who had forfeited the chance to educate themselves through service in the Liberation Army, or in other revolutionary activities.

"It was not just a matter of making education available to all such persons, but also of thinking about those who, without aid in the form of cheap or free housing, or scholarships, would not be able to attend school or university. In certain cases, such people were even given a kind of wage while they studied, so that their families would not suffer from any loss of earning power.

"Nor was our effort centered only on the struggle against

illiteracy, which today has been reduced to the point where half the Chinese people, including most workers and a growing number of peasants, can now read and write. Some 100 million people in all have left the ranks of the illiterate. But our further aim was, and is, the education, on all levels, of the whole Chinese people, so that not one talent would remain undeveloped, not one useful man or woman would be wasted."

The Primary Schools

Many of our talks with the Minister revolved around the all-important theme of primary education. Progress in this field is one of the great accomplishments of the Revolution, for when the masses were lifted out of the state of ignorance in which they had been held, the first step was taken toward formation of the leadership cadre which today constitutes the surest guarantee of China's future.

"The construction of a primary school," the Minister said, "is almost always accompanied by the laying of a cornerstone for a factory, or by preparation of nearby land for an agricultural installation. When the building is completed, our first problem is to facilitate the children's attendance, as well as that of the illiterates—especially women—among the adults. The old Chinese saying, 'In a woman, ignorance is virtue' today makes both old and young peasant women laugh.

"The extraordinary value that the Revolution has placed on the potential contribution of the Chinese woman, once her mental and social development is fully achieved, should be inscribed among the country's great accomplishments. In addition to the women intellectuals and the women who occupy responsible posts in government, many are to be found in factories, engaged in tasks that have assured them national fame. One such case is that of Yi Shih-chuan of State Textile Factory No. 2 in Shanghai, who heads a group of women spinners who have become heroines of labor. Their fame comes from the fact that they completely fulfilled the state plan for eight successive years. Everywhere people talk about Yi's group as a symbol of women's efficiency. And today Yi is a deputy to the National Assembly."

Education: Second Stage

"The second stage in the evolution of our educational system, from 1953 to 1957, coincided with the First Five-Year Plan and the transformation of agriculture, industry and the position of the artisans. It was also the period of a basic transformation of our whole educational set-up.

"There had long prevailed in Chinese education an irrational distribution of studies. Thirty-six percent of university students majored in political science, law, and economics, because their purpose was to prepare for a state post, or to make money. In contrast, the number of students in the faculties of technology or medicine, for whose services the country had far more need, was far smaller. State needs did not count; all that counted was one's own career. It was the sign of colonial influence on education.

"We had to change all that, and began by increasing the number of technological institutions. The result is that at present the student body is distributed more or less as follows: 40 percent in technological institutions; 20 per cent in normal schools preparing for teaching careers; 11 percent in medical schools, and 10 percent in agronomy and reforestation."

"And in law and science?" I asked.

"In law, and in old-style political science, two percent— more than enough. Before there were law suits, and now there are none.

"The imbalance in curricula was not the only major fault we had to rectify. The geographic distribution of the universities was also irrational, having been based largely on the interests of the imperialists. The university had to be in the coastal zone, the business zone of the rich and of the foreigner. Today, however, 50 percent of our universities are in the interior of the country.

"For years, the scarcity of teachers was a major problem. We took advanced students out of their schools and assigned them provisional pedagogical missions, with the understanding that once their missions were completed, they could return to finish their own studies. Many of these students displayed marked ability for teaching, gave up their original vocations, and remained teachers. At the same time, we reorganized the normal schools, increasing their number and raising their quality to a level where today they are equal to universities.

"Unemployed intellectuals also contributed considerably to the task of preparing teachers. At the time of the Liberation, there was a relatively large number of unemployed university graduates who were now given an opportunity to serve their country and to earn a living.

"In all cities and provinces we have special centers where teachers may widen their knowledge by attending advanced courses. The result is very satisfactory. They have developed a competitive feeling which leads them to study well beyond the point required for the simple work of a primary school. The government is so convinced that the future of the country is linked to the future of education at all levels that it has made special efforts to raise the teachers' status in the community. In the past, teachers were neither respected nor encouraged. Today, of the 1,200 deputies in the parliament, 10 percent are teachers.

"Married teachers with large families get a special subsidy. Both their employment and their pensions, on retirement, are assured. In pre-Liberation days the problem was unemployment, a lack of jobs, plus lack of security on the job; today the problem, as I have told you, is just the opposite—a scarcity of teachers."

Education: Third Stage

"The third stage of the educational reform coincided with the beginning of the Second Five-Year Plan and the Great Leap Forward—that is, from 1958 to today. This is the period of the 'cultural revolution,' which consists mainly in encouraging workers to become intellectuals and intellectuals to become workers.

"The purpose of the cultural revolution goes beyond increasing production, although this is not an insignificant aspect. What is sought is a fusion of technology and economy, and a combining of intellectual and manual work to the advantage of both and to the benefit of the nation. In terms of human relations, it means the end of the arrogance of the intellectual class toward the worker. Thus, the educational system is suffused with socialist content.

"From primary school through university, the new concept of education tends to inculcate in the student the 'five loves' enunciated by Chairman Mao: love for the homeland, for the people, for work, for science, and for public property."

I asked the Minister how students participate in the new educational policy.

"In three ways," he replied. "First, they work on questions related to industry or agriculture within the school itself; second, they leave their schools to study problems of production in factories or on the land; third, they participate in community campaigns such as the Health Campaign, the drive to raise production, etc.

"Our experience over a three-year period indicates that, with some rectifications—which we are always ready to make— the policy of the cultural revolution is a correct one. It has broadened the horizons of the students, giving them a first-hand vision of the interdependence of all the activities of the Chinese people. Moreover, the reports we receive from physicians indicate that health has improved with physical labor.

"There is, of course, the other side to the program: to help workers and peasants to become intellectuals—if the word is not too pretentious—and to give them access to higher education. For these purposes, we have established a nation-wide network of educational centers."

The Chinese press abounds in news about workers and peasants who succeeded, within the framework of the policy outlined by the Minister, in becoming professional people. There is the widely publicized case of the carpenter-mathematician, Yu Chen-shan. As a child, Yu was fascinated by the multiplication tables, but since he came from a poor family, he could not go to school until he was fourteen, meanwhile working as a carpenter's apprentice. Later he joined the People's Army in the war against Japan, where he used his mathematical talents by helping his military unit establish correct firing ranges for its cannon. Only after the Liberation, when he was able methodically to take up courses in higher mathematics, could he fully develop his remarkable talents. Today this carpenter has become one of the country's most distinguished mathematicians, a member of the research section of the Department of Mathematics and Mechanics at Hopei University in Tientsin."

I asked the Minister of Education about scientific research.

"Research is carried out through the Academy of Sciences, the various centers of specialized research, and the universities. Cultural exchanges also help to stimulate scientific research. The quality of the work we are doing here greatly interests scientists abroad, who are waiting for the absurd obstacles erected by their governments to disappear in order to invite Chinese scientists to their universities."

We finally touched on the problem of alphabet reform, which I had found to be a burning question when I visited China in 1957, and on which I had read extensively.

"The writing reform poses tremendous problems," the Minister explained, "and they must be solved with great caution. If we were to change the alphabet abruptly," he pointed out, smiling, "we might find ourselves producing illiterates. We would be forcing those whom we have taught to read and write to undo all that they had done.

"For that reason, the reform is being carried out in two stages: first, the simplification of writing, which will facilitate education; second, reducing the number of characters in the alphabet. Even so, five thousand characters will, in a certain sense, be indispensable; but since the old dictionaries contained ten times as many, even this will mean a very great simplification.

"Another problem we face is unification of the dialects. The word 'footwear' for example, has one name in Peking and quite another in the south. And to add to the confusion, what the south calls 'footwear' means 'children' in Peking.

"As for the use of Latin characters, a practical method is being used to enable people to recognize them. They are used on match boxes and in certain illuminated signs, illustrated with drawings, so that they will enter the people's consciousness through their eyes."

My contact with the professors of the University of Peking permitted me to complete the exposition on education given to me by the Minister. The training of teaching personnel has outstripped, in quality and quantity, anything that could have been hoped for from the first two Five-Year Plans. A veritable army of three million instructors, with working-class intellectuals as the core, is involved in the training of teachers, lecturers, and specialists in the fight against illiteracy. Besides the old intellectuals, the majority of this vast legion of educators is made up of young teachers trained under the People's Republic, who alternate the task of teaching the untaught with that of training teachers who will carry on the country's great educational tasks.

Divorce, Chinese Style

It is unusual in China to encounter a divorced man or woman. Divorce is legal; provisions for it were included in the Marriage Law promulgated in 1950, the year after the inauguration of the People's Republic. This law abolished the feudal type of marriage which was based on the concept of the superiority of man over woman. In practice, however, New China frowns upon divorce and, within reasonable limits, may even obstruct it.

A husband cannot ask for a divorce if his wife is pregnant, although a pregnant wife may initiate the action. The tendency in Chinese divorce law is always to protect the woman and child.

A divorce hearing has become an almost obligatory feature of any book on China by a foreign author. In abbreviated form, the procedure runs more or less as follows. The judge-president of the court begins by announcing his name and those of the people's advisers who are seated at each side of him, as well as those of the recording official, the lawyers, and the petitioner. If either of the parties in the case for any reason challenges the objectivity and impartiality of the judge or his advisers, he may, upon presentation of supporting evidence, ask for transfer to another court.

The spouses involved are then identified, and the judge and his advisers proceed to question both about the circumstances that have led to the divorce petition. Let us assume that the complaint is based on ill treatment; the wife says she was beaten by her husband in the course of a dispute, or was the victim of her mother-in-law's meddling. Chinese couples quarrel about the same things that other people do. What is uniquely

Chinese, in Chinese divorce proceedings, is the way in which the court approaches the problem of possible reconciliation.

If the woman is the petitioner, the judge may ask the husband: "Don't you know the law that says that in marriage the parties ought to help each other?" He questions the husband about his reasons for having disregarded the law, emphasizing, if the friction between the couple was due to a difference in the level of education between man and wife, that it was the husband's duty to try to perfect the wife's education and not to treat her as an inferior. "After all," he might say, "the Chinese people have abolished the feudal system for good reasons. The old attitude of believing that the man has privileges which the woman ought not to claim is antiquated and intolerable in the regime and the period in which we live."

If the husband responds to this argument, and begins to admit his share of guilt in the threatened collapse of the marriage, the court starts the work of reconciliation, guiding the palaver between husband and wife which follows. After that, the court retires for consultation and then returns to announce its decision. The advisers and the recording official stand up. An absolute silence gives the moment a solemnity that will remain engraved in the memory of the couple who, "in view of the existence of a possibility of reconciliation, are required to make whatever efforts may be necessary to consolidate their relationship in mutual affection and understanding."

The Administration of Justice

The Vice-President of the Supreme People's Court, Wu Teh-feng, who is also Vice-President of the Chinese Association of Political Science and Law, took time out to give me an over-all idea of what the administration of justice is like in the New China.

"In approaching the present judicial system," Mr. Wu said, "three elements should be kept in mind. First, there are the customs of the Chinese people; second, there is the experience of the revolutionary struggles; and third, there is the consciousness of the masses.

"From the first element, the 'customs' of the ruling class,

which were to dominate and to oppress, are naturally excluded."
Therein, explained Mr. Wu, is a major difference between a
capitalist and communist judicial system. Under capitalism, the
stronger the social consciousness of the people, the harsher the
repression. "But among us, the customs of the people consist
precisely in not tolerating oppression. As a consequence, oppressive measures are eliminated. In socialist countries," he
continued, "the laws and their administration respond to the
social consciousness of the people, instead of violating it. And,
in turn, they inspire the people's consciousness."

Mr. Wu then sketched the general outlines of the Chinese
state. The first article of the Constitution stresses the character
of the leadership, which rests in the working class on the basis
of the worker-peasant alliance. The state, then, is a people's
dictatorship.

It was logical that such a state should confront at once
the problem of putting an end to the abuses of feudal power,
and that its legal decisions would be directed against the land-
owning class and the upper bourgeoisie, who together had kept
the Chinese masses in their formerly miserable condition.

"The possession of democratic rights," Mr. Wu said, "could
not be extended to any of these exploiting elements. And according to the concepts vigorously formulated by Chairman Mao,
we grant these rights only to the people. But the people includes
the national bourgeoisie which, in contrast to the bureaucratic
bourgeoisie, placed itself at the side of the working class during
the democratic revolution."

"The national bourgeoisie," observed the Vice-President of
the Supreme Court, "presented a dual character: revolutionary
and counter-revolutionary. The first led us to strive to win it
over to our side; the second obliged us to take adequate pre-
cautionary measures to avoid a substantial delay in revolutionary
development. Our policy in this respect must have surprised
quite a few people outside of China. But the evidence shows
that, if we had opted for destroying the national bourgeoisie
insteading of winning it over to us, we would not have strengthened the Revolution, but rather its opponents.

"The problem was resolved in a manner which permitted China to move peacefully all the way over into socialism.

"One ought not to forget that the concept of the democratic people's dictatorship is not that of hegemony. In the case of hegemony, the leaders decide everything. But the power of a people's dictatorship rests on the full development and practice of true democracy.

"Bourgeois democracy is proud of its elections. There, the electoral campaigns are very lively, during which many promises are made which frequently are not fulfilled. The fact is that the voters, after being ardently courted, are then abandoned at the altar.

"We believe that democracy should be judged not by its form, but rather by whether, in the last analysis, action is determined by the people or by the heads of government. We are attentive to the will of the people and we design policy in accordance with it. The opinions come from the masses and the government studies, analyzes, synthesizes, and channels them, and gives them the form of decisions. The communes are a clear example of popular initiative."

As another example, Mr. Wu cited the formulation of the Chinese Constitution. That document, he told us, reflects the desires of the people and is a consequence of their revolutionary experience. The draft was submitted to the consideration of the democratic parties and the people's organizations. Amendments were proposed. The text was the subject of a discussion in which more than 150 million Chinese participated, and then it went to the Assembly for approval.

"The same principle," said Mr. Wu, "prevailed in the cooperative movement that culminated in the communes. The Assemblies were the organs that fixed their statutory bases."

The high magistrate explained to us in detail the function of the Assembly in the public life of New China. In each province, the supreme government organ is the People's Assembly; in the districts, the District Assembly. In the region—that is, in today's commune—the supreme organ of power is the Assembly of the members of the commune. "All rights," went on Mr. Wu, "rest in these Assemblies. And those rights are based on the will of the masses. No decisions can be made without taking their will into account."

Mr. Wu now described the functioning of justice. As in other judicial systems, the two main organs are the court and the prosecutor. To arrest a person accused of crime, the prosecutor's consent must be obtained, although a lawbreaker taken in the act may be arrested by anyone and handed over to the "information organ." The latter must then request authorization of the prosecutor within 24 hours in order to maintain the arrest. If the prosecutor denies authorization, the arrested person must be freed.

Unless the crime involves state secrets or illicit sexual relations, the hearing takes place with the greatest possible publicity. In a pre-examination, the decision is made as to whether or not the evidence warrants a trial; if not, the accused is set free.

China's hierarchy of courts runs as follows: districts are served by the basic People's Courts; above them is the Intermediate Court; in the provinces is found the People's Superior Court; and, at the top, is the People's Supreme Court. The rights of appeal are guaranteed. Not only the accused, but also his relatives and friends, may appeal a verdict.

Mr. Wu explained that the court which conducts the first examination is made up of a judge and two jurors; in the court of the second examination, all three members of the court are jurors. Unlike in the West, jurors are elected by the people and have the same right as have judges to question the accused.

In addition to the accused's right to defense counsel, his relatives and friends may enter a defense in his behalf, as well as any organizations of which the accused is a member. Sentences include a mandatory death sentence; a death sentence which may be commuted after a stipulated period of good conduct; life imprisonment; imprisonment graduated in accordance with the gravity of the crime; and probation, which provides that the convicted man is free but is put under the control of the people.

The majority of those found guilty of major crimes have been rehabilitated, according to Mr. Wu. "We have a system of subsidies," he explained, "for relatives of prisoners who are undergoing re-education by labor. A prisoner's family may find itself without means of subsistence. In that case the relatives receive a subsidy from the state."

Re-education through work is carried out in various places, including factories and farms which have educational sections. Thus many criminals have been turned into useful citizens and have been incorporated into the working force. Consequently, the crime rate diminishes from year to year.

Mr. Wu explained why the New China has neither a civil nor a criminal code. "(1) We are in a new, socialist society; the situation changes from day to day, and it is not practical to codify under conditions that would call for constant amendment. (2) Since the foundation of the People's Republic, only a dozen years have passed, and we do not have enough experience of our own, nor can we limit ourselves to copying the codes of other countries. (3) The people feel that a criminal code with a hundred articles and a civil code with a thousand articles would be difficult to understand. They prefer individual decisions and laws. When we have sufficient experience, codification will come."

Oil for China's Lamps

Since our first visit to China, I had been interested in finding out—within the limits imposed by that country's national security—something about its mineral resources and their exploitation. My long talks with the Vice-Minister of Petroleum, Li Jen-chun, and his principal co-workers confirmed my impression that China has a great future as an oil-producing country.

"China," said Mr. Li, "has a past as an oil-producing country, but a fragile one, in keeping with the generally fragile state of its pre-Liberation economy. We began with a limited number of experts in the field. From 1907 to 1949—that is, over a span of more than 40 years—China had developed no more than 18 geologists and 10 geophysicists. We didn't have a single school of geology. True, geologists came here from America, England, Sweden, and Japan, but their interest was limited to the needs of the countries that sent them. In effect, they never bothered to investigate the broader possibilities of our subsoil. And apparently the prospects of quick and easy profits appeared dubious to them and they preferred to adopt the thesis that China was 'a country without petroleum.' We heard as much no longer ago than last year, when some expert expressed a similar point of view in the United States. But that," Mr. Li added, smiling, "has not discouraged us in our work."

After the People's Republic was founded, interest in petroleum mounted as the economy increasingly came under planning, and research and production in oil were intensified with the Great Leap Forward.

"In the first few years," said the Minister, "the cooperation of the USSR was of great value. Our Soviet friends possessed a highly developed petroleum industry and technology. Little by little we began to extend our own cadres, training geologists and experts in our universities and special institutes. Today we have five academies and more than 20 technical schools devoted especially to geology.

"Thus we have learned, first, to estimate realistically China's possibilities in petroleum and, second, to employ the most modern methods of exploration and drilling—for example, the new radioactive and biochemical methods.

"Exploration has proved that we are *not* poor in petroleum. In the past, we had accepted the West's skepticism in this regard, but Chairman Mao's attitude has been completely different. Instead of discouraging the search for oil, he supports it. And at the same time he favors the creation of the technical cadres without which no endeavors, however enthusiastic, can get very far.

"Conscientious and systematic research have made possible a just evaluation of resources and opportunities. Petroleum also needs the support of a strong industry, especially steel. The Great Leap Forward, by strengthening steel production, also promoted the petroleum industry, beginning with the manufacture of the required equipment. An adequate supply of equipment made here in China has freed us from dependence on imports.

"The government places major emphasis on exploration.

We realize that we are still far behind other oil-producing countries. But prospects are good. How do we move forward? The answer is to be found in our social system.

"Petroleum is different from other minerals in the financing of its production. It is necessary to start with ample resources. Capitalists, when they believe an investment in oil may not pay profits, abandon it. The financial incentive must be great for them to persist. Such a problem does not exist under a socialist system. Here work is done not for company profits, but for the people.

"Another problem in capitalist countries is that the land belongs to individuals or corporations. This creates obstacles in the way of exploration that do not exist in China. As soon as we find a favorable location, everyone, beginning with the people's communes, competes in helping us with our task.

"We work here with enthusiasm. In Taklamakan, a famous desert, there prevailed the myth that 'when one entered, he never left.' From 1929 to 1935 some Swedish companies went into the desert looking for oil; they made no progress and abandoned the enterprise. In 1958, we sent an exploratory force into the region. Things were difficult: there was a lack of drinking water, and the winds were fierce. But our force persevered and oil production there is now under way.

"Recently, oil-bearing areas have been found in many parts of China. At this moment, the goals of the Third Five-Year Plan have not yet been set, but it is certain that they will call for a great increase in oil production."

The Political Parties

In addition to the Communist Party, there exist in China today eight political parties, as well as certain extra-party organizations which also cooperate in the reconstruction of the country. The parties are:

The Revolutionary Committee of the Chinese Kuomintang. It was formed in 1948, a year before the Liberation, by democrats who had long opposed Chiang Kai-shek's leadership. They were joined by other progressive elements who, although they recognized the services performed by the Communist Party, did not feel inclined to join it. Among them are to be found people who belonged to the highest class of pre-revolutionary society.

The Democratic League of China. Founded in 1941, it distinguished itself during the war with Japan by its policy of national unity. Later it expelled from its ranks the Youth Party and the National Socialist Party, which could not make up their minds to break with Chiang. In 1947, the Kuomintang declared the League illegal. At present the majority of its members are intellectuals who work in the various scientific or cultural disciplines.

The Chinese Association for Democratic National Construction. Representing mainly the old industrial and commercial class, it was founded in 1945, also as a consequence of a conflict of ideas with the Chiang regime. Its members are patriotic industrialists, the national bourgeoisie to which we have already referred.

The Chinese Association to Inspire Democracy. In 1945 a group of intellectuals, dissatisfied with the weakness of the government in the struggle against Japan, met and founded the Association, which today includes many professors and teachers in the secondary and primary schools.

The Democratic Party of Peasants and Workers. This is the old Revolutionary Party of China, reorganized in 1947. Scientific workers make up most of its membership.

The Chih Kung Tang of China. Its origin goes back to the period of the Secret Societies. It is made up chiefly of overseas Chinese.

The Chiu San Society. Formerly called The Society for Democracy and Science, it was founded in Chungking in 1944 by a group of democratic university students. Its present title means "The Society of the Third of September," and commemorates the victory over the Fascist forces. Among its members are to be found some of the most famous scientists in China.

The Democratic League for the Liberation of Taiwan. It is made up in part of natives of Taiwan who are now living on the mainland.

At a state banquet to which we had been invited, our hosts

had the happy idea of seating us with representatives of the various parties. Numerous toasts were drunk, on this occasion, to the indissoluble friendship of the parties that form the United Democratic Front; and these, together with my conversations with our fellow-guests, increased my desire to delve more deeply into a question about which there is a great deal of misunderstanding abroad, i.e., the role of China's democratic parties and their relation to the Communist Party.

At my request, then, a meeting was arranged for me with Hsu Ti-hsin, an authority on the subject of the United Democratic Front. I asked Mr. Hsu to begin by describing the main characteristics of the Front.

"The United Democratic Front," Mr. Hsu explained, "was formed and acts under the leadership of the working class in its broadest sense—not of the bourgeoisie. Within it, there are two alliances: the worker-peasant alliance and the alliance that includes the national bourgeoisie. There was a close relation between the Front and the objectives of the Revolution and, later, its post-war tasks."

Mr. Hsu then said that certain background information was necessary to an understanding of this organization, and I summarize here what he told me.

The Democratic Revolution was divided into four phases: The first was the revolutionary Civil War, which lasted from 1924 to 1927. Between 1923 and 1924, the question arose of relations with the Kuomintang. Dr. Sun Yat-sen was still alive. "A man of great generosity," noted Mr. Hsu, "and a patriot who possessed a keen sense of the passage of time, he proposed that the Kuomintang collaborate with the Communist Party."

Within the party, which at that time had only been in existence for three years, there were different tendencies. The opportunists of the "Left"—a "Left" in quotation marks, my interlocutor remarked—did not want to work with the Kuomintang, a bourgeois party. At the other extreme, the opportunists of the Right advocated a relationship which would have converted the Communist Party into a kind of affiliate of the Kuomintang.

After many discussions, it was decided that Communist

Party members would join the Kuomintang, but the party as such would retain its identity. In this way, the party aided Sun Yat-sen to reorganize and give new life to the Kuomintang, which now became a mass party and thus changed its character fundamentally.

This was already a United Front, and its formation contributed greatly to the organization of the Revolutionary armed forces. At that time, Chiang commanded the Cadet Corps of Canton. The struggle against the militarists from the North was carried out successfully. By the spring of 1927, the Revolutionary Army had taken control of almost half of China.

But Chiang Kai-shek, helped by American and British interests, began to plot in the ranks of the Kuomintang to assure his own leadership at the expense of the cooperation introduced by the United Front. He became adept in double-dealing. While he was still pretending to be of the Left, he was sent to Moscow to learn military science. But as he became stronger, it became increasingly clear that he represented Rightist elements.

Imperialism was able to use Chiang as its ace in the hole against the Revolution. The ploy was helped by the divisions that prevailed among the Communists, whose right wing had begun to "walk slowly." According to its view, the role of the Party was to pull the cart, and that of the bourgeoisie was to ride inside.

When Chiang reached the Yangtze, the workers and peasants requested two things: arms and agrarian reform. The armed forces of the Revolution could have grown and become irresistible. That Chiang did not want this to happen was, from his point of view, natural. But the Rightists in the Communist Party were not up to the situation either, and permitted the Revolution to fail. With this, the United Front was destroyed.

Mao Tse-tung demonstrated the consequences of that mistaken policy to those militants who were still unable to assimilate the meaning of what had occurred. His ascendancy over the Communist movement and the Chinese revolutionary movement in general dates from that time. He rose to power because of the accuracy of his analysis of cause and effect, and because he convinced his followers of the lack of realism in the position taken by the Party's right wing.

In the second phase of the United Front, Mao's efforts were directed at maintaining unity in the face of the demoralization of the party's Rightists, who saw no alternative other than to give way to Chiang, and the demoralization of the "Left," which demanded a break with everything that was bourgeois.

I asked Mr. Hsu to give me some examples of this second, pseudo-Left tactic, to which he attributed in great part the reverses in the Revolution of 1927. He gave two concrete examples. In the region where the working class dominated and was under the influence of the extreme "Left," it acted in so radical a fashion that small business was ruined. Instead of collaborating with the national bourgeoisie, the latter was antagonized. The second example related to the "Left's" military adventurism. At that time the Kuomintang was dominant militarily. Facing that situation, Mao Tse-tung defended his well-known strategy: to retreat, to pursue, to harass the enemy, but above all to avoid destruction in showy but ineffective offenses. His strategy was finally adopted and, thanks to it the Red Army, though much smaller in numbers, defeated four Kuomintang attacks. But due to the sudden resurgence, in the most exposed sector, of the military adventurism of the "Leftists," a fifth attack succeeded. The result was heavy losses for the revolutionary forces, and the Long March had to be undertaken.

"The national crisis," continued Hsu Ti-Hsin, "heightened when the Japanese occupied the Northeast and threatened the entire North of China. Under the weight of the crisis, the national bourgeoisie began to incline toward the United Front. It was a great opportunity to incorporate it into a framework of patriotic collaboration. The 'Left' opportunists did not see it that way, and they launched the slogan of defending the Soviet Union with arms. The national bourgeoisie replied: 'Go defend the USSR. We are Chinese. What interests us is the struggle against Japan.' Mao Tse-tung took these sentiments into account.

"The third phase of the Democratic Revolution coincided

with the most critical period of the war against Japan. Our forces were inferior to those of the Kuomintang. No matter how repugnant it was for us to cooperate with a party whose main ambition was to destroy us, the need to oppose Japanese aggression came before everything else.

"Therefore, we made a great effort to revive the United Front. It was not easy. It was necessary to do it on the basis of forcing the Kuomintang to fight more resolutely against Japan. But the Kuomintang was showing itself to be more militant against the Chinese Communists than against the Japanese invaders. Nevertheless, the internal contradictions were growing within the bourgeoisie; a part of them clearly wanted to resist Japan and looked with disfavor on the dictatorial tendencies of the Kuomintang.

"Naturally, it was on that sector of the bourgeoisie that we depended, establishing a difference, clear and real, between the frankly reactionary forces and the centrist forces."

Before the war with Japan there existed here, as parties, the Kuomintang; the Communist Party; the Democratic Worker-Peasant Party, composed in part of leftist members of the Kuomintang who were disillusioned with Chiang Kai-shek, and other independent elements; the Youth Party, admirers of Clemenceau; the National Socialist Party, modeled after Hitler's Nazis; and another small group made up of Cantonese and emigrés opposed to Sun Yat-sen, called Chi Kong.

During the war against Japan, other parties arose, such as the Association of the Alliance of Democracy, founded by professors and intellectual patriots (its president, Shen Chun-ju, still active, was 86 years old when we met him), and those groups enumerated earlier in this chapter.

"Again there was a possibility of reviving the United Front," continued Hsu Ti-hsin. "We applied ourselves to the task undiscouraged by past failures.

"We come now to the fourth phase of the Democratic Revolution, which covers the years 1946 to 1949, immediately before the Liberation. After the surrender of Japan the Chinese people were filled with an impatient desire for peace. They had endured almost 105 years of war, beginning with the Opium War and including 20 years of civil strife.

"In 1949 Mao Tse-tung, making himself the spokesman of the demand for peace, went to meet Chiang to arrange for a peace based on negotiation. Pressured by public opinion, Chiang agreed to negotiate and an armistice agreement was reached. But Chiang soon broke the armistice and unleashed a full-scale Civil War. We had no alternative than to counter the Civil War with the War of Liberation.

"The Centrist parties did not believe that the Communist Party could win this struggle; besides, many of their members feared the agrarian reform. Nevertheless, we made every effort to maintain contact with them and to convince them that the agrarian reform was indispensable, and that it would be carried out with equity and prudence. As for the Kuomintang, it used the two parties that it had succeeded in winning over to its side—the Youth Party and the National Socialist Party—to intimidate the other political groups and influence them against any United Front.

"The Centrists wavered; then, unrealistically, offered themselves and their program as a compromise solution to the political impasse. The Communist Party published a statement affirming that the 'third line' advocated by the Centrists was an illusion. But we persisted in maintaining contact with the middle grouping, patiently explaining the issues, and our efforts finally proved effective. Gradually the Centrist parties grew close to the Communist Party and before the Liberation the United Front again became a reality."

Here Hsu Ti-hsin brought up a name which I esteem very highly, that of Chang Hsi-jo, former Minister of Education and President of the Institute of Foreign Affairs. Mr. Chang never belonged to any political party, but, possessed of an extraordinary culture and great authority won in the service of his country, he has been able to serve as a most valuable contact among the various political forces.

The Revolution's fifth phase was opened by the Liberation. Once established, the United Front was consolidated and broadened to cope with the concrete tasks of national reconstruction. It played an important role at the first session of the Consultative Conference, held in September of 1949. This Conference, which carried on the executive functions of the national government until the National Assembly was instituted, considered two essential questions: the elaboration of a Common Program, which for a period served as a constitution, and the designation of a permanent government for the country.

"As you know," Mr. Hsu went on, "since 1954 the National Assembly has been the supreme organ of power. But the Consultative Conference continues to exist as an advisory body and to provide liaison among the parties. The most important questions of policy, domestic and foreign, are submitted to it before going to the National Assembly, which converts its recommendations into laws. The United Front, operating through the Conference, is a working adjunct of government, with a past firmly linked to our revolutionary movement and the Liberation, and not merely—as our enemies state—a 'propaganda gimmick' designed for foreign consumption."

My last talks with Hsu dealt with one of the points upon which I wanted further clarification: how, and to what extent, the democratic parties actually participated in the public life of New China. I had prepared a questionnaire on the subject that I submitted to my amiable and patient informant before I left for the provinces, with the understanding that we would examine it together on my return. When I again saw Mr. Hsu, he had prepared answers to all my questions. To conserve space, I will summarize his answers rather than attempt to give them verbatim.

National Assembly deputies are normally elected by regions. "But this procedure"—here I quote Mr. Hsu textually—"would give almost all of the seats in the Chinese parliament to the Communist Party, thus depriving the democratic parties of representation. So, by mutual agreement, a share of Assembly seats is automatically awarded to the non-Communist parties."

The makeup of the second legislature, covering the period 1959 to 1962, illustrates the effect of this agreement. Of the 1,226 deputies in that legislature, 41.49 percent were members of the various non-Communist groups, including organizations that are neither workers' nor peasants' groups nor part of the Communist Party. Together, these groupings had a total of 514 deputies.

The Permanent Commission of the National Assembly consists of 79 members. During the 1959-1962 period, 39—or 48.98 percent—were from political groupings other than the Communist Party.

During the same period, the Council of State, i.e., the Council of Ministers, had 39 ministers and commissions. Of these, nine—or 23.1 percent—belonged to the democratic parties. One of the most important ministers in the present period of economic "consolidation and readjustment" is Li Tsu-chen, formerly manager of the powerful Wun Li Chemical Company.

As for the National Consultative Conference during the same period, 672—approximately 63 percent—of the total of 1,071 members did not belong to the Communist Party. Of the 158 members who composed the Conference's Permanent Commission, 86—or 54 percent—were non-Communist.

"While the National Assembly is the organ of power," Mr. Hsu said, "the Consultative Conference is an organization of the United Front. The second is very important in fixing the domestic and foreign policy of the country.

"During the period of the Democratic Revolution the Communist Party sought to work with everyone, parties and men, willing to cooperate. In the present period of transition and socialist construction, we are applying the same policy." And he added firmly: "We will continue with our policy of long-range coexistence and mutual control."

The phrase "mutual control" led to a question that I had formulated about a point of particular interest to me. "To what degree," I had asked, "can the democratic parties make their opinions felt and see their demands satisfied, even when these clash with the position of the Communist Party?" I want to reproduce the reply just as I took it down:

"The General Line is the specific responsibility of the Communist Party. But in concrete questions, we make every effort to take the opinions of the other parties into account. And when the Common Program was established, we considered the opinions of the democratic parties, as we did when preparing the Constitution.

"Of course, not all the suggestions offered by the democratic parties are accepted, but the constructive ones are welcomed. For example, there arose in the Consultative Conference certain procedural difficulties which could be traced to the fact that members often lacked knowledge of the subjects under discussion. A Kuomintang deputy, Chang Chi-chung suggested a way in which the deputies could familiarize themselves with the questions they were to consider before the legislative session began. In essence, the proposal was that deputies of both the National Assembly and the Consultative Conference be given the opportunity to visit locations where national projects were under way, so that when the projects came up on the agenda, the legislators would know whereof they spoke. Mr. Chang's proposal was accepted.

"Another example: It was Cheng Chien, Vice-President of the Revolutionary Committee of the Kuomintang, who requested the undertaking of certain important hydroelectric projects on the Yangtze River—projects that are now under way. And a third example: Tan Kah-kee, one of the leaders of the group representing the overseas Chinese, pointed out that Fukien province had not a single foot of railway. Due to Mr. Tan's intervention, the Yin-Tang-Amoy railroad line was built."

At a meeting in honor of the memory of Dr. Sun Yat-sen, which took place a few days after my final talk with Mr. Hsu, I met many of the leaders of the democratic parties, as well as other non-party democrats. At this meeting a woman, Ho Hsiang-ning, life-long revolutionary, noted painter, and Chairman of the Revolutionary Committee of the Kuomintang, gave an enthusiastic speech in praise of the United Front.

The National Minorities

Just as China has provided for fair treatment of its minority political groupings, so too it has applied the principle of egalitarianism to the problem posed by its minority ethnic groups.

In the Palace of Nationalities in Peking I documented myself very carefully on the subject of China's minorities—a subject of particular interest to a Spaniard with a constructive position on the problem of federalism. Mao Tse-tung insisted from the beginning of the revolutionary struggles that the Han nationality, the largest in China, should constitute the center of an egalitarian policy that would slight no minority, however small.

The central government has helped reconstruct the minority languages to make them adequate instruments of communication in the new world these peoples are entering; and it has assured access to all levels of education for masses of people previously doomed to illiteracy. This has been a considerable task, for half of China's 50 minorities had no written language at the time of the Liberation.

Equality of treatment of minorities is proclaimed in China's Constitution. Laws have been passed to encourage development; yet each minority is left free to decide on problems that affect it particularly. Although all minorities together comprise only six percent of China's population, the electoral law gives them ample representation in the national government. Of the 1,226 deputies which constitute the National People's Congress today, 179, or 14.6 percent, represent the national minorities.

The intelligent treatment extended to them by Peking explains the enthusiastic support which the minorities have shown for the New China, and the determination with which they are developing their economies and their cultural and artistic potentials. Twice each year, on the holidays that fall on May 1 and October 1, they parade before the President of the Republic in Peking, resplendent in their national costumes and performing their colorful native dances.

Take the case of Sinkiang, a region of great promise. Minority nationalities embrace a large part of the 4,870,000 inhabitants. The most numerous are the Uighurs, concentrated principally in the south, and comprising 74 percent of the population. All of the minorities, working in harmony, have modernized the hydraulic works in their region, and constructed new ones, thus considerably enlarging the area of cultivated land. The Academy of Science, and the Central Institute of Nationalities, have sent philologists and educators into Sinkiang—as they have done to other regions where minorities live—to help solve the complex problems arising out of the prevalence of dialects.

Tibet

In view of the world-wide interest that the Tibetan question has aroused, I was particularly interested to meet the well-known American writer, Anna Louise Strong, who had recently been in Tibet with a group of correspondents. She told me something of what she had learned from the Tibetans of what the old socio-economic system had been like. Tibetan peasants were serfs then; they worked for their masters "all the hours of the day and all the days of the year." For this they were paid 50 pounds of barley flour a month per head, and some additional grain which, eventually, they might exchange for a pair of shoes. A female serf, if she wished to get married, had to present her master with a coin, tobacco, tea and a *hata,* or ceremonial shawl. Since the serfs received no money for their work, and their pay in grain was insufficient for the gifts with which they had to "buy" their right to get married, engaged couples worked extra hours on separate plots of land so that, at long last, they could be wed.

The whip was the order of the day. A girl was whipped if the wind carried off a handkerchief from the clothesline where it was hung out to dry. A man was whipped if he could not pay his debts to the master.

Miss Strong described how, after the area was liberated by the Chinese, investigating committees confronted many of the former masters with their newly liberated slaves. The latter told hair-raising stories of persecution and suffering. "Nine of my family died at the hands of our masters in two years," one peasant said. And, pointing to his own former master, he cried: "You took all our livestock from us. When my old father protested, you had him given 800 blows with the whip, from which he died. My whole family was destroyed; you confiscated all of their property, and I was thrown out to beg on the roadside."

Yes, according to Miss Strong, even the peasants who had been most cruelly treated did not now ask for their masters' death. Their most common request, shouted into the faces of those who had mistreated them, was: "Confess! Repent! Destroy the old regime! Destroy the torture instruments!"

I saw some of these torture instruments, including cages in which prisoners were held, in the museum of the Palace of Nationalities.

The delegates to the U.N. are free to believe what they are told about the bucolic life in Tibet before the Chinese Revolution, but they would do well first to talk on the subject with some of the Tibetan young people we met on the campuses of several Chinese universities.

The Last Emperor

When, on a hot August morning in 1961, I interviewed in Peking Mr. Pu Yi, as the last Emperor of China is now called, the gentleman was busy writing his memoirs. It was a fascinating interview—and not only because of what was said. The very fact that the former Emperor was alive, that he had survived the Revolution, was itself a significant fact—and to many readers, no doubt, will come as a surprise. But Mr. Pu Yi is not only alive; he is busily enjoying his new role as a writer, which he adopted following the years he had spent as a gardener after the Chou En-lai government had released him from prison.

The simple fact that the former Emperor of China circulates freely in the capital of the New China should serve as one more point to ponder for those who write about that country. A regime that again and again has been described as the most intolerant, extremist, and sectarian in the world can point to its last Emperor living peacefully among his fellow citizens and working, like them, for the progress of the nation.

Pu Yi himself never ceased wondering, during the days following his release, how it could have been possible. "I was fed very well in prison," he told me, "but I thought that was

merely to assure that I would be well nourished when the hour
of my execution arrived, just as cattle are frequently fed heavily
before being taken to the slaughterhouse. And the truth is that I
deserved to be executed. Although I will regret it for the rest of
my life, it is a fact that I committed high treason when I
collaborated with the Japanese invaders."

What follows are a few of the notes that I took during my
long conversation with the former Emperor.

The first part of his narrative was devoted to childhood
memories. He became Emperor at the age of three. That was in
1911, when all the Southern provinces were demanding the
abdication of the Manchus. And then, in effect, he was forced
to abdicate, and became young Pu Yi. He remained a commoner
until the Japanese, who had invaded Manchuria, decided that
his enthronement as Emperor of Manchukuo would serve their
plans. He was crowned Emperor on March 1, 1934, and the
ceremony was carried out with every attention to ancient
tradition.

The Manchu or, as it is officially known, the Ching dynasty,
degenerated as time passed. On the whole, it cannot be compared
with the old, truly Chinese dynasties, headed by poets, painters,
city builders. The Ching dynasty can boast only one really great
Emperor, Kang Hsi, a contemporary of Louis XIV and Peter the
Great, and the equal of either of them. The Empress Dowager,
Tzu Hsi (nicknamed the "old Buddha"), who died when Pu Yi
was two years old, was the last of the Manchu royalty who
holds some interest. She was a dominating, able, astute woman,
as she showed by escaping from the palace disguised as a maid
during the Boxer Rebellion.

Pu Yi, fond of music, gives the impression of being an
intelligent and cultivated man. I was told that his Chinese
teachers had fostered his literary talents and that he is well versed
in the history and philosophies of his land. I particularly enjoyed
hearing him talk about the accomplishments of the New China
and about Chairman Mao in a tone that held neither servility
nor artificiality. He speaks of the New China in tones that reflect
three ancient Chinese traits: respect, serenity, understanding.

I saw the former Emperor again at a banquet celebrating National Day, the anniversary of the Revolution. Pu Yi came with his youngest brother to our table to drink to our health and happiness. He had words of special courtesy for my wife. Moments earlier, we had noted the former Emperor and his brother seated alongside Queen Elizabeth of Belgium.

Pu Yi's memoirs will some day be a best-seller in America, for he knows how to tell his dramatic story exceedingly well.

11

CULTURAL LIFE

The People's Republic attracts many Chinese intellectuals from abroad; some return to stay, while others tour the land, prompted by curiosity mixed with a patriotic impulse. Thus the *Peking Review,* an English-language weekly of great value to those who follow Chinese affairs, mentioned the return to Peking from Hong Kong of the elderly and distinguished pathologist Ho Pao-chang. The weekly quoted Dr. Ho's impressions of the New China at great length.

One of the things that struck Dr. Ho most favorably was the progress in scientific research, especially in medicine. Another was the understanding attitude of the Chinese authorities toward the need for intellectual independence in scientific work. "The policy of allowing 'a hundred flowers to bloom' and a hundred different schools of thought to compete," he said, "has stimulated scientific research and produced positive results." This statement was published in June, 1962, when in other countries it was being said that Mao's famous dictum had been permanently abandoned. Further to this point, a recent editorial from the publication *Red Flag* noted that "It is an error to take a brutal attitude in regard to ideological problems." Yet the people abroad who still refer to "the hundred flowers" thesis as a "passing whim" are the very ones who make fun of the fact that the Faculty of Letters of the University of Peking has introduced a course on existentialism.

In returning to China, Dr. Ho was following a pattern initiated some time earlier by a group of Chinese scientists, headed by Dr. Hsu Shen-tsien, who left universities in the United States to work in the New China at considerable financial sacrifice. At present they occupy pre-eminent posts in their country, and it is to their return to their homeland that American military experts such as General Thomas D. White, former chief of the U.S. Air

Force, attribute China's advances in ballistics and aeronautics, and its preparations for entering the atomic age.

The Chinese have recently revived the tradition of the great encyclopedias. Centuries ago China was far ahead of other countries in learned publications of this kind. Now they have announced several new major works of scholarship, some of which will certainly be translated into English, French and Spanish. They include a three-volume history of Chinese philosophy by Feng Yu-lan, University of Peking professor, who published a work on the same theme 30 years ago; an *Encyclopedia of Mechanics,* directed by Professor Liu, Vice-President of Tsinghua University, who with the aid of the Academy of Sciences and the Ministry of Education, and with the collaboration of his colleagues, is making a study of 9,000 ancient books on machinery and technology; a new history of China by the renowned historian, Chien Po-tsan; and a history of Chinese literature by Yu Kuo-sen in cooperation with young professors from the University of Peking.

The Peking Opera

As is known, the Peking Opera is a multiple art in which singing, dancing, pantomime, and dialogue combine to create the desired effect. Since our last visit, the Peking Opera had lost the great Mei Lan-fang, whom I had the privilege of meeting. At age seventy-four, he was still admirable in the role of Lado Chao in *The Sword of the Universe,* a theatrical work adapted from a novel of the time of the Chin dynasty, a thousand years ago.

Of the generation of great, old Chinese actors, the brilliant Chou Hsin-fang was still active. In December of 1961, he celebrated the sixtieth anniversary of his debut on the stage. For many of the young people, he was the indisputable master, and will doubtless remain so until, like Mei Lan-fang, he decides to retire.

Some foreign observers insist that the Peking Opera really should not be spelled with a capital "O." They argue that it is not an institution, but a theatrical *genre,* and that any group following the same tradition could justifiably call itself "Peking opera" even if it performs in a small, provincial town. Those who take that view propose that the name Peking Opera be changed to Peking Theater. But it appears that few Chinese support this suggestion.

What does cause lively discussion is the content of the Peking Opera. Among communists who specialize in cultural affairs, there are some who resent the fact that its repertory, much of which was created in feudal times, reflects the superstitions and antiquated notions of a feudal society. They resent, too, the occasional "license" with which it treats amorous themes. In part as a reaction to former corruption, the Chinese today reject anything that smacks of pornography or licentiousness. Nor is the frequent glorification, in some Opera works, of imperial heroes acceptable to these critics.

But the immense popularity of the traditional theater in the country, and the great success that the performing companies have had abroad—I witnessed their success in Paris and Berne —have reduced the opposition, limiting it to a task of expurgation. For instance, texts are either changed to suit modern views, or they are offset by others which do not praise some ancient leader or the charms of an imperial concubine, but rather exalt the masses and the men and women who are constructing the New China.

People's Art Theater

The People's Art Theater in Peking is China's finest contemporary achievement in the theatrical field. It brings together many of the most famous actors of the country, and its repertory includes both historical and modern works. In a successful modern play, *Mme. Tsai Wen-chi Returns to Her Native Land,* by Kuo Mo-jo, the best-known intellectual of the present regime, a combination of poetry and prose is utilized for the first time in Chinese drama.

Among works which can be described as modern classics, the repertory includes various of the best plays of the pre-Liberation period, notably *Thunderstorm* and *Sunrise* by Tsao Yu—plays that made their author famous in the 1930's. The theme of both dramas is the search for freedom by the Chinese intellectuals of the period. A foreigner in the theater can follow the play by means of a resumé in English or (often) in Spanish or French.

Today there are more theaters in Peking than in New York, with the further difference that the American theater is likely to be prohibitive for a family with a modest income, while here the working couple with three children who one night sat in front of us, hugely enjoying an encounter between loyal swordsmen and traitors in a thousand-year-old opera, paid something like a dollar for their five seats.

There are now a dozen more movie houses in Peking than there were in 1957. The visitor has no difficulty in spending an evening out in China's capital; the only difficulty is in making a choice among the many possibilities available.

Of the plays that I saw this time, I particularly enjoyed a Peking Opera production, *The Women Generals of the Yang Family,* which paid homage to the valor of the female members of that great house of the Sung dynasty (960-1279). In the service of their Emperor and the homeland, when all the men of the family fell in the war against the invaders, the women raised the banner of resistance despite the defeatism of the War Minister, who wanted to surrender. The women succeeded in persuading the Emperor to continue the war. He gave them command of the armies, and they finally defeated the enemy, freeing China of the threat of foreign occupation.

The uprising organized by the Society of the Small Daggers —about the time of the Taiping Rebellion—is the theme of a film I saw in the Seagull movie studio in Shanghai. I spent an afternoon at the studio with the personnel director and the celebrated actresses, Chin Yi and Hsia Li, both very beautiful, the well known actor, Mo Jan, and the director, Tsen Chun-li, one of the Chinese film makers whose fame has extended abroad.

The movie about the Society of the Small Daggers had just been filmed when we visited the studio, but some revisions were still under consideration. I am sure that had it been released in time to be shown at the World Film Festival which I attended in Moscow in 1961, where a Japanese and a Soviet film divided the laurels, it would have been awarded a prize. Excellently directed, the film reveals the extraordinary progress the Chinese have made in color movies. Making use of the multiple techniques of the national theater—singing, dancing, pantomime and acrobatics—the film tells a story of heroism and love. The time is autumn of 1853; the place, Shanghai. The Society of the Small Daggers attempts an uprising, but is crushed by the ultra-reactionary government, supported by foreign capitalists.

The Chinese Actor

No actor is more well-rounded than the Chinese actor. That is why he is always the very center of the play; the stage director and the rest of the company are eclipsed by the performer. In reality, the *metteur en scène*, or Western-style director or producer, does not fit into the Chinese theatrical scheme of things. The new regime attempted to give him an importance he had never before possessed, using him to produce contemporary works dealing with relatively recent revolutionary themes. But the audience continues to follow the actor, who must be an excellent singer and dancer, as well as pantomimist. The successful performer must also be an acrobat, capable of fascinating the audience with his skill and daring.

The training of actors begins in infancy. Very rigorous for six or seven years, an actor's training continues throughout his career. A visit to the Academy of Dramatic Art enables one to understand the perfection reached by those who today lend luster to the stage. And it explains the "cult" that surrounds the stage greats, such as Mei Lan-fang.

The traditional Chinese actor is stylized down to the last detail. In one of the academies of the Peking Opera, fifty varieties of hand movements are taught. The hands appear and disappear in the long sleeves of the silk robes and may give the performance a delicate touch of femininity or an abrupt gesture of anger. The long beards, the feathers of exotic birds, the hairdos, the weapons—everything is subject to a careful process of stylization. Whether in the companies where all the roles are played by actresses or in those composed only of men, whether in the romantic duo or in the warlike encounter, the players have behind them a discipline of constant and patient rehearsals until they reach perfection. It is a training to which few Western actors would submit. The art, the style, of the actor are more important in many cases than the content of the play he is performing. Nevertheless, the repertory of the Peking Opera is full of themes capable of delighting the discriminating Chinese audiences.

Unlike the situation under the Chiang Kai-shek regime, the competent performers of the New China play important roles not only on the stage, but in the cultural and public life of the country. Many are deputies in the National Assembly. They hold important posts, naturally, in the National Theatrical School. Some actors and actresses earn an annual salary of a thousand yuan or more, higher than that of many members of the government.

Age constitutes no barrier to the Chinese actor. Yu Chen-fei, President of the School of Operatic Art in Shanghai, and himself an excellent actor, told me that during the company's visit to Hong Kong, the Chinese who live there—some of them extremely wealthy and certainly not communists—paid tribute to the change which had taken place in the Chinese theater. He quoted one of them as saying: "In the old society, the old actors and actresses were not worth more than a *cao* [blade of grass], but in the new society they are valued like *bao* [jewels]." Yu told them how 76-year-old Kai Chiao-tien was a sensation in the Peking theaters, and how the sixtieth anniversary of the appearance on the stage of another of the great performers of the Peking Opera, Chou Hsin-fang, was marked by a memorable celebration.

Themes of Drama

It is not easy for modern playwrights to compete with the classics. The history of the Chinese theater includes powerful writers such as Kuan Han-ching, whose seven-hundredth anniversary was celebrated in 1958. The anniversary was marked by performances of his works all over the country; many of his plays are part of the standard repertory. Some of his works are indictments of the Mongol conquerors, their abuses of power, and their infamous treatment of the Chinese. Others deal with simpler, more universal topics. In *The Dream of the Butterflies,* for instance, the wealthy and powerful Ko Piao abuses his power to get rid of all who stand in his way. Among his victims is Wang, a laborer. Wang's three sons plan to avenge him and are arrested. Fortunately, the local prefect is a brave and honest man; but at first he condemns one of the sons. Then he has a dream in which three young butterflies are imprisoned in a spider web; their mother saves the two older butterflies, and sacrifices the youngest. In the real case with which he is confronted, all three brothers declare themselves to be equally guilty. The mother begs the prefect to forgive the two older brothers, and resigns herself to abandon the youngest to the law. Intrigued, the prefect questions the mother and discovers that the two older brothers are the children of Wang's first marriage, while the third, whom she is willing to sacrifice, is her own son. Moved by so much generosity, the prefect frees all three. The despotic master whose conduct had precipitated the tragedy is executed.

In Nanking we saw what can be considered a masterpiece of the modern theater, *The Storm in the Celestial Capital,* put on by the Modern Drama Company of Kiangsu province. It is the history of the Taiping Rebellion.

The first scene is the garden of Tien Wang, the Celestial King. The time is the spring of 1860. The Celestial capital, besieged by the army of the Ching dynasty, is in danger. Tien Wang has called Prince Li Hsiu-chen to the Palace to discuss a plan of attack against the Ching forces. As a result of that interview, the Prince begins to march toward Hangchow. But meanwhile, at the court, vacillations and intrigue triumph, and the Prince is ordered to abandon his preparations for attack.

However, supported by the affection and aid of the people, the Prince refuses to obey and takes Hangchow by force. The court intrigues continue. The King is seen to waver, sometimes in favor of the Prince, other times against him. But the Prince's military successes finally paralyze the palace conspiracies, and the Prince is enabled to lead his soldiers into a victorious, final battle. There is popular rejoicing; the flames of triumph are reflected in the sky. Yesterday's plotters approach Li Hsiu-chen one after the other. The Prince confounds them with a smile.

At the International Film Festival in Moscow I discovered in Yu Lan, who plays the mother in *A Revolutionary Family,* a performer of extraordinary talent. She won the award as best actress. Sharing Yu Lan's popularity on the Chinese screen are three other actresses: Chin Yi (*A Tai Doctor*), Wang Yu-chen (*The Red Guards of Lake Hunghu*), and Chu Hsi-chuan (*The Red Women's Detachment,* a prize-winning film).

Films based on the war and the Revolution continue to be the most popular in China, and *The Red Women's Detachment* is an excellent example of the *genre*. Its theme is the heroic conduct of the women of Hainan who, in response to the Communist Party's appeal for equal rights for women, enrolled in the revolutionary struggle on the side of the people.

The party's appeal is heard by the heroine, Kiong-hua, a serf exploited by a local despot. From that time on, Kiong-hua thinks only of escape. She tries to flee, is caught and punished, and is subsequently given as a gift to an "important merchant" who has made an unexpected visit to her master. The girl meets another young woman who is in a similar situation, and after a series of adventures while crossing the forest, both finally reach the revolutionary base where a woman's military unit is under training. There, Kiong-hua not only discovers women of a kind she has never before known, but also sees the "important merchant" who had freed her and who turns out to be the local delegate of the Communist Party.

In broad outline, the story is true: Kiong-hua was one of the authentic heroines of the revolutionary struggle in the 1930's. The role offered Chou Hsi-chuan, a relative newcomer to the screen, the chance to give a performance that made her a star overnight. We saw the movie in one of those provincial theaters where the audience is particularly enthusiastic. Such audiences wait for months for a film to reach them. They know what it is about from press and radio reviews, and when it comes they watch it in a silence so profound that we felt guilty every time our Chinese companion helped us with an explanation of the plot.

Among the most active studios in China is Shanghai's Seagull, mentioned earlier in these pages. It is one of the country's oldest film centers. Two separate studios were located on this spot 30 years ago. With these and others, the basis was established for more ambitious projects, until in the summer of 1957 the government decided to raise the unit to the rank of a "production studio" and enabled it to obtain the required material.

At the outset, the equipment was poor: half-broken sound machines, only two cameras, and space for staging one-fifth of what it is today. With equipment from the USSR, the studio began to practice sound recording. Pre-Liberation China had produced none of its own movie equipment. "Today," said Mme. Hsi Shen-chu, the capable director who has made many excellent documentaries, "we have our own film-equipment industry."

From 1958 to 1960, the studio produced many outstanding films. "It was our Great Leap Forward," as director Tsen Chun-li put it. Among Seagull's noted films were *A Permanent Spring in the Time of the Flowers*, *The Patriotic Mandarin*, *The Tai Doctor*, *Song of Victory on the Shores of the River*, *The Basketball Player*, and *The Railway Workers' Guerrilla Group*.

"We encourage variety in theme," said Mme. Hsi. "Naturally we pay a great deal of attention to the subjects related to socialist construction. Art for art's sake, detached from the present state of mind of the masses and from national reality, would mean falling into artificiality. But we also produce films designed to popularize the study of history, and we have made others based on themes by writers who, no matter in what period they wrote, reflected the deepest sentiments of the Chinese people. We are partisans of the 'hundred flowers' policy not only because it is just, but because it guarantees that our artistic production will not succumb to tedious conformity."

Out of the Past

One of the things that disconcerts some foreign visitors who are not particularly aware of the meaning of the Chinese Revolution, is the link everywhere apparent between past and present. Men whom the world considers to be the most rigid and doctrinaire of communist leaders treasure this link. One reason for this is that China, throughout its long history, has produced many personalities of a strong revolutionary nature. These personalities, and the history of their times, furnish the Chinese stage and screen with an inexhaustible supply of dramatic material.

There was the case of Emperor Yu, the engineer-ruler of the Bronze Age, who essayed the control of the rivers and who, as ruler, felt himself obliged to be so constantly at the service of his people that he had a bell placed where his poorest subject could toll it and make his complaints heard.

There were the monarchs of the Tang dynasty (618 to 907 A.D., one of the greatest dynasties in China's history, under which the poets, among them Tu Fu, exerted a major influence on public life. The rulers felt that poets were worthy of being heard in the highest and most powerful circles.

Both the Sung dynasty, renowned for its painting, and the Ming dynasty, famous for its ceramics, were notable also because, from king or emperor down, leaders emerged who devoted themselves to revolutionizing the practices of government for the advancement of the country and the well-being of the common people.

Emperors such as Shen Tsung (1071) declared they considered the happiness of the masses more important than the profits of the wealthy. Some rulers came from peasant families, or in any case not from the nobility, as did Kao Tsu of the Han dynasty (206 B.C. to 220 A.D.). On three occasions, an emperor of peasant origin was the founder of a dynasty.

Under many emperors, the court felt that its worth should be measured by the importance it gave to "things of the spirit." The eleventh century was notable for the growth and power achieved by intellectual "elites." Contributing to this cultural expansion were the development of printing, which stimulated reading from one end of the country to the other, the creation of philosophical and literary schools, and the study of the classics. In the twelfth century, the spread of science and technology added to the intellectual ferment. New types of rice and other plants, and new methods of cultivation, revolutionized the countryside.

The Sung dynasty, again, was one of artistic creation,

handing down to posterity the glorious works of Li Lung-mien, painter of beautiful horses. Under the Ming dynasty, in the sixteenth and seventeenth centuries, dramatic art predominated. Some of the plays of that period are produced today.

Throughout the centuries, there appear heroes and heroines whose courageous conduct in the frequent struggles against invaders won them the undying admiration of the Chinese people. And mass movements, mainly among the peasants, who sometimes rebelled against foreign aggression and sometimes against the internal feudal system, are still recalled with pride.

This past, so rich in events of such variety, is kept alive by the Chinese theater and films. Since the inauguration of the new regime, the various culture departments of the People's Republic have been given encouragement and support so that the classic theater, led by the Peking Opera, may enter a new period of brilliance. Works unearthed from the archives have been incorporated into the repertory and are received with enthusiasm by the public. The wisest of modern leaders are not afraid that a drama extolling the energetic Yung Lo, third emperor of the Ming dynasty (1368-1644), who refused to consider the old silk route to the West as the only safe commercial route and sent the fabulous Cheng Ho the Sailor across the seas, will awaken monarchical sentiments in the Chinese of today.

The film directors, for their part, transfer to the screen some theatrical productions of the classic *genre,* together with episodes from the long anti-colonial and peasant struggle of the period from the middle of the nineteenth to the beginning of the twentieth cenuries.

Song of Sungs

Among the most intellectual ruling families, the Sung dynasty has every right to a pre-eminent place. Chinese scholars who, as we have noted, put the merits of culture far above military glory, were delighted with the coming to power of this dynasty. Instead of attempting to repeat the military victories of the Han and Tang dynasties, the Sung rulers favored a return to rigorous classicism and the cultivation of letters. Philosophical speculation again made its appearance—this without neglect of the people's material well-being and the need for wide social reform.

Under the Sungs, the most controversial personality of his time, and undoubtedly the most vigorous, was Wang An-shih. This eleventh century reformer worked above all for the strengthening of the state. The people's welfare interested him mainly because he felt that a happy and industrious people would contribute more to the general prosperity and to the treasury. It was natural that with such ideas, he would direct his greatest efforts toward agriculture, the basis of the Chinese economy of the time.

Wang An-shih's reforms did not include redistribution of land; the great estates were left intact. But there was a redistribution of financial responsibilities, and he introduced a system of price controls over agricultural produce. This was probably as far as he could go at the time.

The Sung dynasty did not neglect the arts. At an exposition organized in October, 1961, to commemorate the tenth anniversary of the Revolution, we saw some of the best paintings of the Sung period, several of whose emperors were artists of talent. One of them, Hui Tsung, was famous as a painter of birds and flowers and was considered the best art collector of his time.

Of all China's great dynasties, the Sung dynasty is most likely to interest the person who can take time to turn his attention toward the past. Numerous evidences of its genius are scattered among the museums of the country and in the antique shops. It embellishes with extraordinarily delicate shades the old Chinese culture as a whole.

The Sung emperors surrounded themselves with the best artists, who were often lodged in the palace. The emperor considered it an honor to copy the poems he most liked, sometimes illustrating them himself and sometimes leaving that task to the painters. Each transfer of the court meant that the poets and painters would go along; thus the new place chosen for the capital would be converted into a museum city and literary center. From this period date the works of Ma Yuan, some of which are in the Boston museum, and of his son, Ma Lin. Painting, like scholarship, was likely to run in the family.

Painting and Literature

Modern Chinese painting is not very different from the old, as far as themes are concerned; contemporary canvases are not necessarily "socialist." One of the best of today's painters, Wu Tso-jen, inscribes his pictures in the classic fashion with his own motto, as for example: "I have walked through all the peaks, but I am still not old." His special field is birds and animals. His black swan is beautiful, and his eagles rule over those mountains through which he has never ceased to wander in search of the violent winter nightfalls and the soft sunsets of spring.

In current literature, revolutionary reminiscences received new impetus in 1957 with the celebration of the thirteenth anniversary of the People's Liberation Army. No less than 13,000 memoirs, amounting to 40 million words, arrived at the central offices of the army over a three-year period.

As for biography, though certain veterans of the Communist Party, Chu Teh, Tung Pi-wu, Hsieh Chueh-tsai, and Wu Yu-chang, were the subjects of recent books, almost no leader of today, with the exception of Mao Tse-tung, has been so honored. Of the non-communist personalities who were "precursors" of the Revolution, two are the constant objects of praise: Sun Yat-sen and the father of Chinese contemporary literature, Lu Hsun.

The memory of Sun Yat-sen is treated in the New China with immense respect and esteem. Kuo Mo-jo, president of the Chinese Academy of Science, published a poem glorifying the man who climbed from peasant poverty to the leadership of the nation. Dr. Sun, like many other great Chinese leaders, had a hard childhood. His widow often recalls the fact that he walked over the hills with bare feet until he was fifteen years old. Before that, he had never even owned a pair of shoes. His family lived in a hut, and their diet consisted mainly of sweet potatoes. But the beauty of his native countryside compensated for much hardship. The road to Macao, today a great highway, is surrounded by mountains and splendid forests; these scenes of Sun Yat-sen's childhood are for his comrades and successors a kind of civic sanctuary.

Chairman Mao, despite his enormous political responsibilities, still finds time not only to write poetry, but to follow closely the literary and artistic activities of the country. It is due to him, according to some of our Chinese writer friends, that a rigid and narrow cultural dogmatism has been avoided. On the occasion of the twentieth anniversary of the Yenan Forum, an assembly of writers held in May, 1942, when China was in the fifth year of the war against Japan, Mao reaffirmed his position, maintaining that "our criticism must permit free competition among all the varieties of artistic work." He insisted that content, form, theme, method of creation, and style, must necessarily be varied. To put obstacles in the path of initiative and creative capacity, he argued, can be highly prejudicial to the development of literature and art.

Recently the literary sectarians were again called to order in public, this time by Pa Chin, a writer who adopted the line of the "hundred flowers" and appealed to his fellow writers to put themselves firmly on the side of independence in creative literary work.

Music and Ballet

During our first visit to China, the Peking Opera absorbed most of the nights we devoted to the theater; this time we attended, in addition to other operas, a number of ballets and concerts.

The China of the dynasties had maintained court orchestras from time immemorial—that is, for more than 3,000 years. Gradually, the enjoyment of music spread to listeners beyond the closed palace audiences. The Chinese love music, and Westerners can follow Chinese music with pleasure after it has been heard a few times. In the Shanghai Music Academy we were told that, thanks to research, the variety of instruments had lately been increased by 200 types of ancient or newly developed ones.

As in the theater, the desire to explore the past dominates Chinese musical activity today. The patience displayed in this effort approaches the unbelievable. For example, the musical historian Yang Ying-liu years ago undertook to revive a musical work left by a famous poet and composer, Chiang Po-shih of the Sung Dynasty. The manuscript was available, but there was no one capable of reading the system of notation. Yang Ying-liu began a careful search in Sian, examining every surviving fragment of evidence until he finally discovered the system of notation that had been employed. Thus a musical composition 700 years old was rescued and incorporated into today's musical repertory.

Music in Shanghai

A music center par excellence, Shanghai is proud of its famed spring music festivals. Pianists like Li Ming-chiang, a brilliant interpreter of Chopin, who has won honors in several international festivals, and singers such as Chu Hsu-fang, a former serf from Tibet, have studied in the city's conservatory.

And there is a brilliant group of young composers. Among them Tseng Chia-ching, whose work, *The Marriage of a Goddess,* in four movements for an orchestra composed of traditional instruments, has been very successful. Of the composers of major works, Ting Shan-teh, composer of a symphony entitled *The Long March,* is much esteemed. He drew inspiration directly from the places where the epic took place, in the southwestern and northeastern provinces, and incorporated into his work some of the songs and dances of the national minorities who live in the territories through which the Red Army passed.

Another symphonic poem which often appears on musical programs is *Monument to the Heroes of the People,* composed by Chu Wei, a veteran of the Red Army.

The Conservatory, while retaining its prestige, is extending its sphere of action. It has trained the majority of Chinese orchestra conductors, who are increasingly in demand, even in areas where previously folklore was the only form of art known. In some of the more important factories that we visited on our trip through the interior, we found amateur orchestras organized by workers, both men and women, capable of performing works from the classical repertory. Occasionally such groups have as their director a fellow worker who studied music at the Shanghai Conservatory during his off hours.

Of course, that is an exception. Future Chinese conductors have to dedicate themselves exclusively to the study of music and undergo rigorous training in the Conservatory. The vast building can handle more than 600 students in all areas of music—theory and composition, national music, piano, singing, orchestral music, orchestra conducting.

At the Conservatory a foreign visitor can enjoy a lesson given with patience and spirit on the Chinese guitar or *p'i p'a*; the two-string viol or *ehr hu*; the shrill trumpet or *so na;* the *sheng,* a small bamboo organ; and the cymbals and drums. All of these instruments delighted us in the Peking Opera performances.

The success of the companies that go abroad has contributed to an increased interest in cultural exchanges. The most prominent orchestra conductors and artists have returned to China impressed by what they have seen and eager to enrich their own work. Latin American and Spanish music, both very popular, have been added to the old programs. "What I would give to sing some day in a liberated Madrid!" a charming Chinese girl, first-prize winner at the Conservatory, told me. And she smiled delightedly when I told her that that day was surely not far off.

The Poet Tu Fu

The golden age of Chinese poetry is ascribed by today's critics to the Tang dynasty (seventh to tenth centuries). In 1962, the country's writers rendered a fervent tribute to Tu Fu, the great realistic poet of that period. He was one of the eight cultural figures of the world chosen for commemoration that year by the World Peace Council, and, appropriately, it was the poet's 1,250th birthday.

Biographical data available shows that Tu Fu spent his youth very comfortably under the protection extended by the court to writers who showed promise. But the period of official benevolence was not to last long. To insure a secure position for the time he needed to develop his talent, Tu Fu was appointed to an official post at the age of 35 and transferred to the capital, which was then Tchangan (now Sian) in Shensi province, and which still preserves the vestiges of its lordly past.

Tu Fu was fascinated by Sian. As visitors there in 1957, we could understand the poet's admiration for a landscape that included Li Shan, a magnificent mountain peak just outside the city. Famous for its curative hot springs, the mountain was the favorite recreation spot of the emperors of the Chou, Chin, Han, and Tang dynasties. Today, thanks to the government's initative, seven sanitariums, built especially for workers, care for more than 8,000 workers every year.

Beginning with the collapse of the Tang dynasty, Tu Fu's prospects went into a decline. Wars had become endemic and the poet was one of their victims. As a war prisoner, he was the tormented witness of his people's sufferings. The experience turned him into a revolutionary writer. From the poems by Tu Fu published for the commemoration in 1962—an occasion that constituted another proof of the interest displayed by the present regime in keeping alive the culture of the past—I have picked out a few brief passages to illustrate the poet's resentment toward the injustices of his period. He wrote on one occasion: "Haughty officials prance on gallant steeds after feasting to their fill, while in the homes of the poor there is no money to buy yarn for weaving." Another example: "While there comes the reek of wines and meats that rot inside the gates of these rich, the bones of the starving and cold are strewn along the roadsides."

And from Tu Fu's celebrated poem, *Song of the Autumn Wind and the Straw Hut*: "Wondering in my dream whether it would be possible to build an immense house with thousands of rooms, where all who needed could take welcome shelter; a mansion as solid as a hill, not fearing wind or rain; then thinking how, if only such could be, would I be content to see my poor hut demolished, and I myself frozen to death." (The translations are by Rewi Alley.)

Safeguarding Antiquities

In 1957, the director of the Peking Library showed us many Chinese incunabula rescued from the greed of invading powers and foreign collectors. Saving the treasures in the museums, libraries, and Buddhist temples has been one of the preoccupations of the new regime. A perfect example of foreign rapacity occurred during the period of Japanese aggression. The Japanese took not only whatever they could of China's mineral resources, but also the most valuable paintings and books.

In Hong Kong stands one of the most beautiful temples in China, the Pagoda of the Heavenly Arch, built during the Ming dynasty. Its collection of engravings on wood of Buddhist images is unique; nothing comparable exists in any of the collections abroad. In the spring of 1942 units of the Japanese army operating in the vicinity of Hong Kong planned to assault the Pagoda. The plan failed, thanks to the intervention of the Red Eighth Army whose soldiers, tipped off by the superior of the monastery, carried away 150 baskets of *objets d'art*. Monks provided yards of coarse cloth for wrapping, so that the treasures would be protected against dampness. Hidden in an abandoned coal mine, the invaluable collection remained safe until the liberation of Peking permitted its recovery and removal to the library. Some of the Buddhist writings had been damaged, however, and experts spent long hours and days restoring more than 3,000 volumes to their original condition.

Interest in Spanish

A great deal of Western writing is being translated into Chinese. On the occasion of Dickens' 150th birthday, a new collection of his best works was put on sale. The interest in Spanish guarantees that in the very near future more translations of Spanish and Latin American authors will be published. As an old enthusiast of Benito Pérez Galdós, I had the satisfaction of learning that a selection from his *National Episodes,* one of the masterpieces of Spanish literature, is to be translated into Chinese.

It was extraordinary to see how the study of Spanish had been advanced in the space of four years. Aside from the high-ranking personnel in the Institute of Foreign Affairs, I want to mention particularly our translators and guides, Mr. Tang Ming-sin, Mme. Wang Zue-jen, and Miss Si Lie-lin, who outdid themselves in helping us at every step.

Tang is an enthusiast of the Spanish language and culture.

It is almost incredible how, without leaving China, he has succeeded in acquiring such a mastery of the language. Modest as are these young Chinese, who are trying to develop competent groups of translators for the service of their country, Tang attributes the excellence of his Spanish to his teacher, Maria Lecea. She and a half-dozen other Spanish refugees are working in Peking in the foreign-language section. We spent a whole night talking to them about Spanish problems and China's interest in them.

Talent Alone Counts

It is not rare to encounter, in today's China, a person holding down a responsible post in a factory or commune who only a couple of years ago was an unskilled laborer or peasant. To win national pre-eminence after a humble beginning is nothing new in China, as many instances cited in these pages have shown clearly enough. But while in China's past, only one out of millions had an opportunity to rise above his station, today millions can rise from the depths of the mines or from the rice fields to become qualified engineers or agronomists. The cultural life of the country is open to all, and the millions of copies of books that are printed—books which only twenty years ago would have had only a small number of readers—show how prodigiously the desire for knowledge has increased.

However, the newcomers to China's professional and intellectual circles offer no threat to the veterans. Age is no impediment to success in the New China, with its profound respect for experience and tradition, and its devotion to a culture that has been transmitted through untold generations. Hsu Teh-li, at 85, is a member of the Central Committee of the Communist Party; Wu Yu-chang, only a year younger, is also a member and is President of the Commission for the Reform of Writing and Rector of the People's University of China—three jobs that would tax the ability of most men half his age.

As long as his physical strength continues, and he retains his mental alertness, the aged Chinese intellectual is not put away on the shelf, as happens so often in the West. On the contrary, his contributions to the national reconstruction are warmly welcomed.

A Minor Art

The ancient art of carving seals has been revived, and today seals are made of bronze, jade, agate, ivory, and bamboo root. It is a craft with a very old tradition. The first official seals appeared under the Chou dynasty 2,500 years ago, but they increased in importance during the Chin and Han dynasties, when they began to be used as certifications. Their possession demanded extreme vigilance on the part of the official charged with their protection; their loss cost him, at the very least, his job.

The taste for carved seals has survived and many Chinese today have their names engraved on seals, which are used to legalize letters, contracts, and documents of all kinds. There are seals of the most varied forms and sizes imaginable, although none is as large as those used by feudal emperors—huge jade seals, some of them weighing more than six pounds, and now on display in museums.

Seal engravers, like penmen, form an integral part of China's cultural life, surviving triumphantly from century to century as part of the tradition of a great people.

12

CHINA TRIUMPHS

Toward the end of 1962, at a time when the Western press was full of reports that China was foundering in the midst of crisis, the speech of Premier Chou En-lai on the occasion of the national festival of the First of October was awaited with special interest. His international prestige is considerable; and even in the chancelleries which are least friendly toward Peking, he is considered a first-class statesman. His style is elevated and free of arrogance; he is candid, courageous and confident in his utterances, and displays a serenity that can spring only from a spirit that is at peace with itself.

"The Chinese people advance bravely and with complete confidence toward the goals which they have fixed for themselves," the Premier began his speech. "The readjustments of the national economy have produced notable results. The economy as a whole has improved since 1960, and that improvement has been maintained from year to year. . . . Contrary to the calculations of the imperialists, the reactionaries of various countries, and the modern revisionists, the Chinese people have become not weaker but stronger."

The Premier analyzed the accomplishments of the 13 years of the new regime, putting at the top of the list two which he considered fundamental: the socialist revolution and socialist reconstruction. "The socialist system," he said, "has been resolutely established in China. A preliminary but solid basis has been created on which to build a vast, modern, and independent national economy. If today's situation is compared with that of thirteen years ago, it can be said that a change like a great earthquake has taken place in China.

"It is," the speaker continued, "the result of the strenuous efforts of the Chinese people under the direction of the 'three red banners': the General Line of the Party, the Great Leap

Forward and the People's Communes." In view of what much of the world had been saying about the Great Leap Forward and the communes, Chou En-lai's emphasis upon them as two continuing pillars of government policy was especially significant.

The Premier spoke of the difficulties encountered in the preceding few years. "As with other revolutionary causes, the work of socialist construction by the Chinese people has not always been smooth sailing. The natural disasters of the years 1959 to 1961, together with the failures and errors in work, have led to difficult situations. But the Chinese are a revolutionary people, with a firm will, and in the past they have never bowed before difficulties no matter how formidable. In accordance with the teachings of Mao Tse-tung, the Chinese people scorned the difficulties strategically, took full account of them tactically, and turned them into an impelling force for advancement. The facts show that the Chinese people have endured the test well. The readjustments in the national economy are proving to be effective."

Chou En-lai's speech was preceded by a communique reporting on the plenary session of the Communist Party, under the chairmanship of Mao Tse-tung, that had been held in Peking on September 24-27, 1962. The *People's Daily* published the communique under the significant headline: "To Consolidate the Collective Economy of the People's Communes and to Develop Agricultural Production."

The Premier's address at the First of October Festival ought to be considered as a kind of addendum to a report he had made some months earlier before the spring session of the National People's Congress. Such reports are customary, and cover developments between sessions of the Congress. It is important to summarize this one, even if only in broad outline, because it was given after the "difficult years" and enables us to see clearly what China can hope for in the course of its Third Five-Year Plan, scheduled to end in 1967.

Analyzing the country's situation as of the moment, Chou En-lai proclaimed the validity of the General Line, which consisted of employing all the forces of the nation in the building of socialism on the basis of the following fourfold production aims: quantity, rapidity, quality, and economy. He stressed that the People's Communes, "established in vast rural regions of our country," have shown "a healthy and constant growth."

It is not the practice of the Premier—as I had discovered when I talked to him in 1957—to slough off difficulties and failures, and he did not do so now as he reviewed government operations in detail. Then he proceeded to lay down a ten-point program designed to assure China's continuous advance toward a solid and *independent* economy. (The stress given to the word "independent" was not accidental.) Here is the program:

(1) To work toward increasing agricultural production, principally in cereals, cotton, and oleaginous products.

(2) To adopt, with relation to heavy and light industry, measures which are reasonable and advisable, giving special importance to the manufacture of consumer goods.

(3) To utilize materials, equipment, and manpower to the fullest—and where they are most needed.

(4) To reduce the urban population and the number of factory and office workers, persuading those who have come from the country to return to their homes in order to strengthen the agricultural front.

(5) To make an inventory of stocks and to review the budgets of each enterprise so that unused material and funds can be transferred to wherever they are required.

(6) To make certain that the purchases of merchandise are properly carried out and to improve the methods of supplying the market.

(7) To fulfill the goals assigned to foreign trade.

(8) To readjust and raise the character and quality of work in the spheres of culture, public health, education, and research in both pure and applied science.

(9) To apply firmly and fully the policy of identifying the nation with the economy, getting the cooperation of everyone in the campaign to reduce production costs and increase incomes.

(10) To continue to improve planning in order to establish and maintain a general equilibrium among the different branches

of the economy, while respecting the following order of priorities: agriculture, light industry, heavy industry.

So much for the future. For the present, the Premier included in his report a statement that brought a sigh of relief from his audience: it was already possible, he said, to announce "a change in the economic situation for the better." Evidently, reports had already reached him that the prospects for the next harvest were excellent—an exceptionally important piece of news for China after a series of lean years.

Thus China's response to those lean years—years so full of trouble that one cannot guess to what end they might have led any other people—was the reiteration of a determination to construct socialism on the basis of a modernized agriculture, modern industry, and ever-greater cultural and scientific endeavors. This is the dominating orientation of the Third Five-Year Plan, the importance of which will be truly extraordinary.

That 1962 session of the National Congress received only limited attention in foreign newspapers, whose interest in the proceedings disappeared as soon as it became clear that the "purges" forecast by some commentators abroad would not materialize. However, the session did have the effect of moderating widespread predictions of further deterioration in conditions in China. It also served to clarify Peking's position on peaceful coexistence. In the preceding months, most foreign observers had been presenting China as belligerent, fundamentally interested only in developing its military power. That opinion was held by Averell Harriman, former President Kennedy's adviser on Asian affairs, among others.

The Congress agenda ended with an affirmation of China's desire to contribute to the cause of peace, but stressing its particular point of view, i.e., that situations could arise in which "a retreat before the forces of aggression, instead of serving peace, would endanger it by giving new encouragement to those aggressive forces by making them believe that they could force new retreats from the socialist powers." In this connection, the Premier defined China's foreign policy:

"China has firmly and consistently developed her relations of friendship, mutual aid, and cooperation with the Soviet Union and other fraternal socialist countries. And it tends at the same time toward a policy of peaceful coexistence with countries which have a different social system."

Contradictory U.S. Attitudes

The opinion of the Americans about the stability of the Peking regime does not concern China's leaders unduly. In my conversations with Chinese foreign-policy experts, I was impressed by their knowledge of world events, and especially of the American scene. They were thoroughly familiar with the men who make policy in Washington, as well as the important American press and radio journalists. Though they had never been to the United States, and I had lived there many years, I could not consider myself better informed about America than they.

These experts greeted with smiles—smiles of amusement rather than resentment—the contradictions they noted in American commentaries on China, which one day predicted its collapse and the next presented it as a power preparing to take over the world. They noted, for instance, that on one occasion C. L. Sulzberger, noted foreign-affairs writer for *The New York Times,* commenting on the discussion which had been taking place in China on the problem of birth control, mixed everything into his commentary—calories, reports of bad crops, failures in the industrialization policy—and arrived at the conclusion that for several years it was unlikely that China could show the dynamism necessary for expansion. Yet the very next day official circles in Washington were expressing alarm because China appeared close to acquiring its own nuclear bomb—a supposition involving a level of industrial development hardly consistent with Mr. Sulzberger's gloomy appraisal of China's situation.

According to another American commentator, the fact that China was so near to making a nuclear bomb was what led Washington and London to seek a nuclear test-ban agreement as quickly as possible. They hoped that such an agreement would block China's entry into the nuclear club. Similarly, a high official of the U.S. disarmament agency thought that China would very shortly be ready to explode a nuclear device, citing the fact as justification for the sudden upsurge of American interest in achieving a test-ban treaty.

The Foreign Press

The manner of reporting on China varies greatly among the various important Western newspapers and magazines. In the British press, one sometimes finds articles written with considerable objectivity. In *Le Monde* of Paris, whose authority in international affairs is generally recognized, René Dumont, professor of Comparative Agriculture at the Paris Institute of Agronomy, wrote after a recent visit to China: "Without the active and voluntary participation of the majority of the Chinese people, the mountains would not have been transformed into cultivatable land, nor would the stones have been carried, sack by sack, from the banks of the rivers. My impression is that the Chinese Communist Party has succeeded in establishing its authority with the consent and the cooperation of the peasants."

Sir Herbert Read, also an authority on Asiatic questions, wrote in *Eastern Horizon* that the well-being of the peasants deserved to receive more attention than production statistics. But if one insists on talking about statistics, he wrote, it can be demonstrated that the Chinese peasants' standard of living has increased fourfold since the Liberation.

This statement is entirely correct. Even during the worst period, from 1959 to the middle of 1962, the Chinese peasant lived better than he had for centuries—better than he had lived, more recently, under Chiang Kai-shek's regime, which was indifferent to the problem of agriculture and, in addition, was shockingly ineffective. All one has to do is to listen to those peasants of the communes who are old enough to remember, tell what their lives had been like under Chiang's free-enterprise system. My notebooks document the differences with an abundance of detail.

In the autumn of 1962 Clare McDermott, Peking correspondent for Reuters, the British news agency, ended his two-year assignment in China with an article in which he summarized the feelings about China harbored by many Western diplomats accredited to Peking. From McDermott's report, it was clear that some of the diplomats differed sharply with their home governments in their estimates of China's future. Their residence in the country had given them an awareness, impossible to more distant observers, of the Communist regime's ability to overcome the gravest difficulties. They felt that New China's 13-year record of achievement should not be underestimated, and that people abroad should be informed of the situation in China, no matter how disagreeable the truth might be for American and Western ears.

The Reuters correspondent repeated certain statements— some made privately, others publicly—by high Chinese officials to the resident diplomats which were, in effect, warnings against any downgrading of China's prospects. The officials did not want governments abroad that might have been unduly impressed by the unfavorable aspects of China's situation to venture into generalizations that would shortly be contradicted by production figures. Without minimizing the problems still to be solved, the Chinese officials managed to convince some of the diplomats that China had "turned the corner" during 1962 and was entering a new period of progress. McDermott himself believed this to be true.

In support of the argument, there was evidence that certain factories, several of which we had visited, were not only making progress in the quality of their products, but were also contributing on a large scale to the formation of highly trained personnel. Factory engineers, in their off hours, were instructing workers as to the results of their own experiments. In this way, the knowledge of the experts was combined with the experience of the workers. Later, in each shop, the workers competed in applying to their daily tasks what the engineers had taught them. The factory was thus converted into a permanent technical school.

One cannot over-emphasize the importance that the creation of ever-increasing trained cadres will have in the coming years. This is true in industry as well as in agriculture and scientific research. In the last analysis, a good part of China's future is linked to progress in culture and education for the masses. Already the country is turning out technicians by the hundreds of thousands.

The Reuters correspondent ended his article by noting that foreign observers believed the new economic measures were already producing positive results and that confidence in Peking was returning as the process of consolidation and readjustment advanced.

The Famine Myth

In *The Other Side of the River,* Edgar Snow's monumental work on Red China today, the author includes a chapter on "Facts About Food in China." In this chapter, he tells how, while he was in China gathering material for his book, he received a series of messages from *Look* magazine asking him to report on the prevailing famine. "I diligently searched, without success, for starving people or beggars to photograph," Snow told his readers: "I realize that the belief in mass starvation in China is now so widespread as a result of cold-war press indoctrination that statements by actual eyewitnesses may be dismissed as wholly irrelevant. Nevertheless, I must assert that I saw no starving people in China, nothing that looked like old-time famine. . . ." In support of his own conclusions, Snow cited observations made by Gilbert Etienne, the Swiss economist on the staff of the School of International Studies at Geneva, and Dr. Armand Forel, a member of the Swiss Federal Assembly. Dr. Forel, on his return from China in 1962, told Snow that he was "allowed to roam the streets freely, saw nothing to indicate starvation, no begging, and one case of rickets."

Snow emphasized the difference between starvation and the scarcity of food that, in China, "is nothing new." He recalled an eminent Chinese scholar who had noted that "between 108 B.C. and 1911 A.D. there were 1,828 famines, or one almost every year." And he gave a series of up-to-date agricultural production figures that agreed with those in my notebooks. He went on to say:

In the best year of her history, in 1958, China probably exceeded American cereal output, running at low speed. . . . But comparisons between China and the United States—which alone accounts for nearly half the world's exports of grain—are less significant than comparisons between China and other less-favored nations. . . . No Communist country anywhere had produced anything like what Marxists call "food abundance." Over the whole decade 1949-59, China appears to have made more progress in that direction than Russia was able to make, despite its greater natural wealth, during the first 33 years of socialism. . . . Nor did Tito's "other road to socialism" in Yugoslavia, where most farmland has remained under private ownership, show results to impress China. In 1962 the Yugoslavs were warned to prepare for a "harvest so bad that it could almost classify as a disaster." . . . China's food supply has steadily improved compared to that of India.

Snow did not consider the problem of the development of Chinese agriculture, seen in perspective, to be as dark as did most of his American colleagues. But as the year 1962 advanced, even these heralds of failure had to modify their opinions. "Mao's China Today: Hungry But No Collapse in Sight" was the headline over a report on China which appeared in the American magazine *Newsweek* (Sept. 3, 1962). "Mao's great leap did achieve a major step toward industrializing an abysmally backward nation," said the article. "In its first year, 1958, China passed Britain and Germany to become the world's third biggest coal producer (270 million tons). Iron-ore production doubled in 1958 and doubled again in 1959 (20 million tons). Previously imported goods like trucks and tractors began rolling off assembly lines."

These figures provided no revelation for us, but it was interesting that they should appear in an American publication which is essentially anti-Chinese, and whose editors could not have been happy about printing them. The report naturally emphasized China's difficulties in providing food, but it admitted that the Peking authorities had had the courage to recognize this publicly. The report quoted Chen Yi, Minister of Foreign Affairs, who around that time had stated that the food shortage was "severe." The quote referred to the summer of 1962, before the first favorable news had come about the next harvest.

On the problem of freedom for intellectuals, *Newsweek*

wrote: "The intellectuals, too, both Confucian scholars and medical technicians, have been given greater freedom—and an increased ration." And the article quoted, as an illustration of the prevailing atmosphere, from a piece which had appeared in the *People's Daily*. The quotation: "All leading cadres [Communist officials] should try their best to avoid arrogance and complacency. . . . We cannot demand that all comrades possess only one view. . . . The emergence of different opinions is inevitable."

But what particularly deserves attention was the closing observation in the *Newsweek* report: "After one or two good harvests, the way will again be clear for Mao or his heirs to order another 'great leap'—this time from a far greater industrial base than before. And when China does leap, the earth will tremble."

"From a far greater industrial base"—in that phrase *Newsweek* summed up the principal aim of Chinese policy: to build an industrial base so firm that it will permit the country, within a relatively brief period, to mechanize its agriculture; to increase the production of consumer goods; to multiply the production of steel, pig iron, coal, and petroleum; to enter fully the domain of atomic energy; to broaden exports. In a word, to do everything necessary to create a nation able to defy any attempt to isolate it, or to force it to remain in the category of "underdeveloped" states.

Emigration and Immigration

Toward the middle of 1962 a great deal was made in the Western press of fugitives from China "pouring into Hong Kong." They were presented as unmanageable mobs fleeing from famine conditions. But nobody wrote about those regions of China which, by tradition, were regions of emigration—and from which emigration had stopped because of improved conditions. For instance, the traditional flow of emigrants from the "district of the sweet potato," as Kwangtung was long called because its soil would grow precious little else, had suddenly ceased. The reason? The miserable villages of the province were being revitalized, its potato-growing land transformed into flourishing rice fields. The construction of adequate irrigation systems had performed this near-miracle. And the fact is that many of the inhabitants of Kwangtung today are people who once lived abroad and have now returned to their birthplace.

So the flow toward Hong Kong had as counterpoint a flow in the opposite direction, comprising people returning to their homeland from various countries abroad, drawn by the promise of the New China.

The Upsurge Continues

As I write this, I have before me many communications from China in the form of newspapers, official documents, and many letters from friends, indicating that the economic improvement noted in 1962 has continued uninterruptedly through 1963 and 1964.

Item. In September of 1962, a friend wrote that the harvests in the northern part of the country had turned out much better than expected. "Honan," he noted, "is having a tremendous harvest. The grain prices are falling rapidly. . . . Meat and eggs in abundance make rationing cards unnecessary." The situation was the same, he said, in Shantung and Manchuria, both of which had suffered severe droughts the previous year. "With all this good news from the northern regions," he added, "the tension has been diminishing from day to day. Of course, the effects of the prolonged bad period which we have undergone must still be overcome, and this will take some time. . . ."

Item. Here is a summarized progress report for 1962 by Yung Lung-kuei, the planner whose discussions with me were related in Chaper Seven:

"In 1962 the national economy was in a slightly better condition than in 1961. The supply of basic articles has increased and prices have remained practically stable. Harvests for the year showed a gain over the preceding year. The goals for industry were achieved: in 1962 everything needed for agriculture was produced, including chemical fertilizers, farm machinery, and tractors. Light industry and artisans increased production by one-third for the first eight months of 1962 compared with the same period the preceding year.

"It is our belief that the recent economic difficulties China experienced are quite different from the economic crises of capitalism. In the capitalist system, crises are inherent; they occur periodically and cannot be avoided. Our problems, arising along the path of progress, can be overcome as we learn by experience. ... Our basic policy continues to be that of regarding agriculture as the foundation and industry as the leading factor in the development of the national economy. The importance given to agriculture does not mean that we mean to make China an exclusively agricultural country. We make industry the leading factor because only with a powerful industry can we overcome our country's traditional backwardness and turn it into a modern nation. . . ."

Item. The National Conference of Agriculture met in Peking in the latter half of November, 1962, and expressed confidence that the agricultural goals for the Third Five-Year Plan, which was to begin with the advent of 1963, would be met. Said Minister of Agriculture Liao Lu-yen, summing up the debate: "The over-all situation in the countryside is good, better than in previous years, and its continued improvement can be counted on." Characteristically, while the prevailing tone at the conference was one of optimism, a good deal was said about deficiencies still to be met—the shortage of tractors and of chemical fertilizers, problems affecting crop selections and the perfecting of agricultural technology.

Item. Together with official statements, letters reaching me from Peking friends who are, by nature, extremely candid, indicated that all through 1963 China's economy continued to improve. Further, the summer of that year provided dramatic evidence that the flood-control and irrigation measures which were described earlier in these pages were well designed and could do the job they were built to do. In mid-summer, Peking was drenched by terrible rains that lasted a week; nevertheless, the People's Communes in the area held up well and continued to ship vegetables and fruits into the half-drowned city. Other parts of China also suffered from the heavy downpours, but the harvests were saved.

The communes did well, almost without exception, all over

the country. The Western press had better forget its notion that the communes are dead as an institution, that they are only being kept "barely alive" for prestige purposes. Far from being dead, the communes have been revitalized and reconstituted. One big change has been to increase their number while decreasing their individual size. At one time, for example, there were 20,000 communes, each averaging around 5,000 families. By 1963 the total of communes had been increased to 74,000, but the average size had been reduced to 1,800 families.

Item. The cessation of Soviet aid has slowed, but has not stopped, the steady progress of China's industrialization. At the end of 1963, reports from the various industrial areas were most encouraging: from Anshan, pride of the Chinese metallurgical workers; from the Wuhan Iron and Steel works; from the factories of Shanghai and Tientsin; from the light industry of Sinkiang; from the oil regions, where the production of petroleum was increasing beyond the planners' calculations. And there was a boom in the pharmaceutical industry, with a dozen factories making penicillin, streptomycin, syntomycin, aureomycin, terramycin and other antibiotics—all of which had previously been imported.

Item. China's economic recovery has led to increasing interest in its markets on the part of many Western countries, especially Great Britain. In August, 1963, the London *Daily Express* reported that "contracts worth millions of pounds for steel, machinery, and machine tools are now being made with China by leading British firms." By the middle of 1963, China had placed more than $5.5 millions in steel orders with British firms. After a visit to London by a Chinese delegation, some 20 British manufacturers signed contracts with the China National Machinery Import and Export Corporation. The British—despite Washington's displeasure—also sold China some Viscount planes. Canada helped to solve its grain surplus by renewing its contract to sell wheat to China.

A British friend who was in Peking in 1963, and attended the festivities commemorating the fourteenth anniversary of the Revolution, wrote to me that there had been in China that year "a much better harvest, plentiful food, and a great enthusiasm and confidence. . . . Despite the raging controversy [the Sino-Soviet dispute], the Chinese are very relaxed and very optimistic."

Item. Raymond Scheyven, former Belgian Minister of Economics, made a fact-finding tour of China in 1963 which convinced him that "most people in the West have grave misconceptions about the Chinese mainland." He listed as myths the Western beliefs that: (1) the Chinese people are worse off under the Communists than they were before; (2) as a result of the Chinese-Soviet ideological quarrel, Communist China will be isolated from the rest of the world; and (3) most Chinese, yearning for freedom, eventually will rise in revolt against their totalitarian government.

Item. In the fall of 1963, the National People's Congress, foregathering in Peking, stressed that "brilliant victories" had been won on the domestic front. So confident was Chinese officialdom in the country's progress that Foreign Minister Chen Yi invited the ambassadors and other diplomats of the 38 countries then represented at Peking to tour the province of Anhwei, which before the Liberation had been one of the most backward provinces of China.

The tour of Africa made by Premier Chou En-lai and Marshal Chen Yi was further evidence that the Peking regime felt secure about domestic developments; the trip would hardly have been made otherwise. The Premier took advantage of his swing through Africa to clarify once more China's position on the question of war and peace. Marshal Chen Yi summarized the position as follows: (1) China needs peace, not war; (2) peace can be secured only through the combined and constant efforts of the world's peoples; (3) it is possible to avoid war, but the danger of one, launched by imperialism, remains; (4) the struggle against imperialism of the peoples of Asia, Africa, and Latin America constitutes a most important factor in favor of peace; (5) if imperialism instigates war, it will be imperialism that will be destroyed, not mankind.

The importance of this African tour was seen clearly in Western chancelleries. Many Western diplomats regarded it as the start of a new phase in China's postwar history. Every major power with an interest in Africa now saw that isolating China would not be as easy as it had appeared—and saw, equally clearly, that a new and powerful element had been introduced into the African arena.

France and the U.S.

The big diplomatic development of 1964, of course, was de Gaulle's recognition of the Peking regime. The consequences were only beginning to be seen as 1964 drew to a close. That trade with France will grow apace goes without saying. So will trade with the nations of the French African bloc. Politically, the recognition meant a rift in the Western powers that must inevitably further weaken the anti-Peking bloc—and not only in the United Nations. Whatever his motives, de Gaulle has strengthened Peking's hand in the enormously complicated international situation which, as this is written, seems to be turning old allies into enemies and old enemies into allies—at least of a sort.

Further, de Gaulle's move accented the bankruptcy of American policy toward China. Washington's attempts to prevent trade between the West and China again proved futile. What can one say of a situation in which France, ostensibly an American ally, permits the leading department store of Paris to put on a Chinese fashion show to encourage the purchase of Chinese goods? And other nations have begun to compete for Chinese trade—Belgium and Argentina, among others. And at the U.N., de Gaulle was pressing the African states of French origin, which in the past had voted steadily with the United States on all issues affecting China, to change their tactics. Sooner or later, with or without the American vote, China will become a member of the United Nations.

The bankruptcy of American policy toward China has been further highlighted by the Sino-Soviet rift. A British businessman, returning to London from China recently, was quoted in the *Sunday Times* of London as saying, "China never wants to be reduced to total dependence on Russia again." This means that great opportunities are in the offing for Western business, and so long as the U.S. refuses to export so much as a match box to China, the plum lies in the grasp of the European nations.

China now trades with 110 nations and has cultural ties with 163 countries and regions. Edgar Faure, former French Premier whose visit to China in early 1964 was regarded in many quarters as a harbinger of French recognition of Peking, reported that a kind of competition was developing among the countries of the West to obtain the benefits that the growing Chinese market would produce for them in the near future. Yet the United States, greatest business competitor of them all, is staying out of this competition.

But aside from trade and international politics, there is something else that the United States—and the rest of the world —ought to weigh carefully with regard to China. "The attempt of some countries to control the destinies of the world thanks to their monopoly of atomic arms," Kuo Mo-jo, president of the Chinese Academy of Science, said recently, "will be crushed in the very near future." One of China's greatest scholars would not speak in this way were he not convinced that China had its foot on the threshold of the nuclear age—and the nuclear bomb.

The Future

In the long run, the fate of a nation depends upon its people and its leadership. The unity and sense of realism of China's leadership is one of that country's most powerful assets. In 1962, when the sessions of the National People's Congress were prolonged and an aura of secrecy seemed to hover over its deliberations, most foreign observers predicted that a great purge was in the offing. Nothing like that happened; and anyone who knew anything about the New China could have forecast that it would not happen. China's leaders are loyal to each other and to their cause, and they are free enough to make whatever adjustments and corrections are called for in the work of socialist reconstruction. Yet they need never worry about maneuvers on the flank by any oppositionist group. And that is of great importance.

Another element on which confidence in China's future can be based is the balance that the Chinese people strike between pride in what they have accomplished and their "wisdom"— something very Chinese—which does not let them lose their sense of proportion. When the Chinese downed the U-2 plane in

September, 1962, Minister of Defense Lin Piao published an order of the day congratulating those who had shot it down—and coupled his congratulations with words which said, in effect, "Don't let my congratulations go to your head." Similarly General Liu Ya-lou warned the heroes of the day against "any feeling of disproportionate pride."

Until those who write or talk about China understand the spirit with which the Chinese people are carrying out the great task they have assigned themselves, they will proceed from error to error. A quarter of a century ago, Japan took advantage of China's period of greatest weakness to throw itself upon its neighbor with the rapacity and brutality of a Prussian military machine. In that test, the steel was tempered—the unyielding spirit that controls and inspires China's present efforts. There is a margin for error in the New China; but there is no margin for surrender.

China still has a great many problems to solve. But for me there is no doubt: China is winning its revolutionary struggle. On many levels, in fundamental aspects of its gigantic, self-appointed task, it has already triumphed.